T.L. OSB

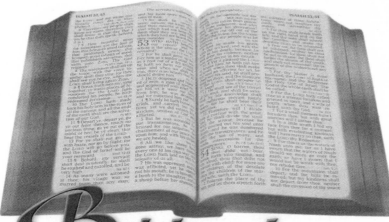

Biblical
HEALING

BOOKS BY THE OSBORNS

BELIEVERS IN ACTION—*Apostolic–Rejuvenating*

BIBLICAL HEALING—*Seven Miracle Keys*
4 Visions–60+ yrs. of Proof–324 Merged Bible Vs.

FIVE CHOICES FOR WOMEN WHO WIN
21st Century Options

GOD'S BIG PICTURE—*An Impelling Gospel Classic*

GOD'S LOVE PLAN—*The Awesome Discovery*

HEALING THE SICK—*A Living Classic*

JESUS & WOMEN—*Big Questions Answered*

LIFE–TRIUMPH OVER TRAGEDY (WHY)
A True Story of Life After Death

MIRACLES-PROOF of God's Love

NEW LIFE FOR WOMEN—*Reality Refocused*

NEW MIRACLE LIFE NOW—*For Asia and The World*
A Global Communiqué of The Christian Faith

PEACE IS A LIFESTYLE—*Truths for Crisis Times*

SOULWINNING—*Outside The Sanctuary*
A Classic on Biblical Christianity & Human Dignity

THE BEST OF LIFE—*Seven Energizing Dynamics*

THE GOOD LIFE—*A Mini-Bible School–1,467 Ref.*

THE GOSPEL ACCORDING TO T.L. & DAISY
Their Life & World Ministry–510 pg. Pictorial

THE MESSAGE THAT WORKS
T.L.'s Revealing Manifesto on Biblical Faith

THE POWER OF POSITIVE DESIRE
An Invigorating Faith Perspective

THE WOMAN BELIEVER—*Awareness of God's Design*

WOMAN WITHOUT LIMITS
Unmuzzled—Unfettered—Unimpeded

WOMEN & SELF-ESTEEM—*Divine Royalty Unrestrained*

YOU ARE GOD'S BEST—*Transforming Life Discoveries*

OSBORN
Ministries
International

USA HQ:
OSBORN MINISTRIES, INT'L
P.O. Box 10, Tulsa, OK 74102 USA

T.L. OSBORN, FOUNDER
LADONNA OSBORN, CEO

Tel: 918/743-6231
Fax: 918/749-0339   E-Mail: ministry@osborn.org
www.osborn.org

Canada: Box 281, Adelaide St. Post Sta., Toronto M5C 2J4
England: Box 148, Birmingham B3 2LG
(A Registered Charity)

BIBLE QUOTATIONS IN THIS BOOK MAY BE PER-
SONALIZED, PARAPHRASED, ABRIDGED OR CONFORMED
TO THE *PERSON* AND *TENSE* OF THEIR CONTEXT IN ORDER
TO FOSTER CLARITY AND INDIVIDUAL APPLICATION.
VARIOUS LANGUAGE TRANSLATIONS AND VERSIONS
HAVE BEEN CONSIDERED. BIBLICAL REFERENCES ENABLE
THE READER TO COMPARE THE PASSAGES WITH HIS OR
HER OWN BIBLE.

THE AUTHOR

ISBN 978-0-87943-143-3
Copyright 2004 by LaDonna C. Osborn
Printed in USA 2011-09
All Rights Reserved

CONTENTS

I DEDICATE THIS BOOK

To THOSE WHO suffer sickness or disease and desire to be healed by God's divine love and power; to those for whom medical science may offer no hope of recovery;

To those who want to know the promises of God for healing and who desire health in order to be at their best for God and for others;

To Christian believers in Java, Indonesia who, during our mass gospel crusade in 1954, first inspired me to publish these truths so that they could be made accessible to the public;

And to the treasured memory of Daisy Washburn Osborn, my beloved wife for nearly 54 years, who co-founded the OSBORN INT'L ministry with its worldwide soulwinning outreaches and who was my associate minister in sharing the gospel with millions, face to face in nearly eighty nations, and whose collaboration, counsel and creative editing, were indispensable to the preparation of this book.

—T.L. Osborn

T.L. Osborn

LaDonna–Age 2 | LaDonna with parents in Javanese *Betja* | Dr. LaDonna Osborn

Introduction

By LaDonna Osborn, D. Min.
CEO, Osborn Ministries International

WHEN I WAS ONLY two years old, I wanted to be a preacher and to pray for the healing of people. In 1954, while riding in a *betja* with my parents in Java, Indonesia, I was glad we were helping people to know about Jesus. In 1947, the year I was born, my parents launched their global mass miracle ministry. We traveled as a family from nation to nation, erecting platforms on open fields, inviting multitudes to come and receive BIBLICAL HEALING. We believed that Jesus of the Bible *is the same yesterday, today and forever.*

Those platforms became *"holy places"* where wonders of God were demonstrated amidst the hurting peoples of our world. As a child, I sat in awe as I witnessed cripples walking, blind people receiving sight, deaf people being restored, cancers and tumors disappearing, and tormented lives being transformed by God's love and grace.

- The *pattern* was always the same.
- The *procedure* was simple.
- The *preaching* focused on Jesus.
- The *presence* of God was manifested.
- The *power* of the gospel was confirmed.
- The *proof* of Christ's life was undeniable.
- The *people* believed the gospel.
- The *purpose* of God's love was revealed.

Miracles are not mysterious phenomena bestowed upon a select few. Nor are they occasional wonders performed by specially gifted intermediaries. Miracles are the life of Jesus Christ being manifested in hurting and disenfranchised people.

Throughout my lifetime, I have been an eyewitness of the signs, miracles and wonders which have been wrought in our mass miracle crusades.

My father is constantly urged to share the secrets that have brought such success to the Osborn global ministry during over six decades. The truths set forth in this book are the essence of what we have taught to people of practically every major religion. They have produced the same results in every nation.

BIBLICAL HEALING shares the seven simple but dynamic truths that *create* miraculous healing in one's life. As you read these pages, do not *try* to build your faith. Do not *try* to be healed. Just read and learn and joyfully ponder these truths. They will do their work in your life. A farmer does not *try* to make the seed grow. He sows it in good soil. *The seed grows by itself.* Jesus said, *The seed is the word of God.*^{Lu.8:11} He is the living word — the *Truth* that sets you free. Just read and as the seed of truth penetrates the soil of your life, your harvest of healing will result.

The miracles and wonders that I have witnessed for so many years, have not taken place because of special prayers or special anointing, but because the seed of the word of God has been sown in the hearts of the people.

> *The life of God in the seed of His word produces its healing wonders in the people.*

I am witnessing the same miracles in the mass crusades that I now conduct abroad, because I am sowing the seeds of the same gospel in the hearts of this generation. THESE TRUTHS, LIKE GOOD SEEDS, WORK LIKE MIRACLES!

I am honored to introduce to this generation, for this century, this revised and enlarged edition that my father has entitled BIBLICAL HEALING. We are convinced that the fundamentals set forth here will bring miraculous healing to thousands of people, as they have for the past half-century.

These seven biblical truths will:

- Unlock your limitations,
- Penetrate your thinking,
- Expand your understanding,
- Excite your hope,
- Dissolve your fear,
- Simplify your perspective,
- Expose your enemy,
- Inspire your faith, and
- Transform your life.

I am preaching and teaching these truths on every continent where I minister. Lives are being transformed by the thousands. Sick and suffering people are being healed. Faith, hope and love are being created in the hearts of multitudes because:

> *The day of miracles has not passed, and Jesus has not changed.*

As you read these pages, expect to experience the BIBLICAL HEALING that has been received by so many others throughout the world.

❧

Preface

DURING MORE THAN a half century of mass miracle evangelism in almost 80 nations, my late wife, Daisy, and I ministered the gospel together and prayed for hundreds of thousands of people who sought healing for their diseases. We witnessed every kind of miracle imaginable, including dead persons restored to life and lepers cleansed by God's power and love.

She and I are the ones who pioneered the idea of mass prayer for mass miracles as the most practical way to minister God's healing love to multitudes in *non*-Christian countries.

We were the first persons since Bible days to go out on fields, in parks or stadiums — in nations abroad, preaching and *publicly praying for physical miracles to prove that the Bible is true and that Jesus is alive and real.* We invited *non*-Christians to come and hear and see for themselves whether or not these things are true.

We did that because of our heart-breaking experience as young missionaries. In 1945 we went to India but did not understand miracles. We were unable to convince the Hindu and Moslem people that Christ is alive and unchanged today.

That experience almost ended our ministry. We were desperate for a way to convince the people of other religions about Jesus and the Bible. During that crisis, the Lord revealed His living presence to us in a vision. This experience re-confirmed to us that we had more than a dead religion. Jesus is a *Living Savior*.

Then we learned about apostolic miracles and, within a few months, we returned to carry the gospel to *non*-Christian nations. This time everything was different. *The Lord worked with us, confirming the word with signs following.*[Mk.16:20]

Our full story is published in our 512 page pictorial, THE GOSPEL ACCORDING TO T.L. & DAISY.

In nation after nation, throughout Central and South America, the Caribbean nations, Japan, Indonesia, Thailand, Africa, India, across Europe, England, Canada and the USA, we have ministered to multitudes of from twenty thousand to a quarter of a million people. Scores of thousands of souls have been saved, many thousands of new churches have resulted, and biblical signs, miracles and wonders have always given proof of the gospel that we proclaimed during over a half-century of global miracle evangelism.

From the time that we discovered that miracles are the answer to convincing the *non*-Christian world about Christ, we always announced publicly that if Christ is alive, as the Bible teaches, then we can pray and expect Him to do the same wonders that He did before He was crucified; but that if He is only a historic, religious figure, then His name will have no power in prayer, nor will He do wonders today as He did in Bible days.

That biblical concept ignited a worldwide renaissance of apostolic faith for physical miracles to confirm the gospel. It affected significant changes in church and global missionary policies, influencing many thousands of gospel ministers to rediscover the power of simple faith in action among the *un*-evangelized millions of our world.

We had written our first book, *Healing the Sick And Casting Out Devils* in 1949. But for these vital truths to be translated into other languages, we realized that they needed to be outlined in a way that could be translated with clarity, and that anyone in any language could comprehend.

During our historic crusades among the Muslims of Indonesia in 1954, Javanese believers urged us to put our teachings into book form so that they could be shared with thousands of others who could not attend the meetings. We did that and this book was first published in the *Indonesian* language. Since then, it has become our most translated book in nations around the world.

Jesus said, *Ye shall know the truth, and the truth*

*shall make you free.*Jn.8:32 Whether spoken audibly or expressed in print, *truth* has the same seed-power and accomplishes the same results. That is why so many thousands of people have been miraculously healed while reading these pages.

In many cases, those who need God's miracle power do not understand the biblical facts that create faith for His blessings.

The seven parts of this book outline the simple truths that we have taught to millions face to face and that have brought healing to hundreds of thousands of people worldwide.

Usually those who pray without receiving the desired response from Christ, lack knowledge of what the Bible says about God's blessings. Without knowing these truths, one has no basis for faith. The Bible says, *Faith comes by hearing the word of God.*Rom.10:17

Hundreds have expressed that after praying for healing, without results, they received a miracle from God when they learned, through this book, what the Bible says about faith and prayer.

A deaf man, unable to hear the teaching, came to one of our meetings. I gave him a copy of this book along with a personal note urging him to read it to help him to have faith, then to come back for prayer. He was so disappointed by this delay that we proceeded to pray for his healing without him understanding the truths on which biblical faith is based. But when his ears did not open, he returned home very despondent.

Two days later, the man returned to our meeting rejoicing, and with perfect hearing. He said that as he read the pages of the book, he received a new living faith, and was instantly healed of his deafness.

Biblical faith is simply expecting God to do what you know that He promised. Without knowing His promises, a person's faith has no foundation. Faith comes by knowing God's promises. Rom.10:17 That is the purpose of this book. His promises are fulfilled in one's life when a person believes them and puts their faith into action.

So, read these pages reverently. Be conscious of Christ's living presence. When we love Him and seek Him, He promises: *I will love you, and will manifest* [reveal] *myself to you...and...will come to you, and make my abode with you.* Jn.14:21,23

The last three chapters of this book make it an apostolic record of gospel ministry. Chapter 24, *Four Vital Visions*, relates the life-changing experiences that catapulted us from the pulpit of a local community to the platforms of global mass miracle evangelism. These spiritual events have never been published before.

Chapter 25 may be the most remarkable record of healing miracles that has yet been chronicled for posterity. More than fifty years of *signs, wonders and miracles* are catalogued. Despite the enormity of our half-century journal, this chapter is limited to glimpses — only *single* days of a *few* of the crusades which usually spanned from ten days to five weeks. The size of this *Witness* required that *dozens of cities* and *entire years* cannot even be mentioned in the record.

Chapter 26 documents the glorious *finale* of this truly *biblical* book, expressed in a unique compendium of 324 Bible verses that have been catalogued, abridged, paraphrased, personalized and merged to express the *Healing Ministry of Jesus Christ* in our modern epoch of time.

These final chapters that climax the teaching content of this book make it a spiritual treasury of biblical proportions. Like John, *we bear record of the Word of God, and of the testimony of Jesus Christ, and of the things that we have seen.*Rev.1:2 *We...testify of these things and have written these things: and we know that our testimony is true.*Jn.21:24

—T.L. Osborn

Chapter 1

Christ—The Miracle Life

HERE IS ONE of the most vital statements in the Bible:

> *Jesus Christ is the same yesterday, and today, and forever.*[Heb.13:8]

This is the Jesus who walked the shores of Galilee, who healed the sick, cleansed the lepers, and raised the dead.

This is the Jesus who forgave sinners and relieved the oppressed. He is the Son of God who *came into this world to save sinners.*[1Tim.1:15; Lu.19:10] His power is the same. His ministry is unchanged.

God wants us to believe that whatever the Lord did for people then, He will do for us today. He who walked the shores of Galilee, is walking by our side in life, today.

He is with us to heal us if we are sick, to save us if we are unconverted, to relieve us if we are oppressed, to help us if we are in need.

The compassion of Christ for those who suffer is unchanged today. He who blessed the poor and forgave sinners in Bible days, is still the savior for us today.

People Then—People Now

• If people could come to Christ and receive His mercy in Bible days, you and I can come to Him and receive His mercy today.

• If God's promises were good in Bible days, His promises are good for us today.

• If a leper could fall down before Him and receive healing then,[Mk.1:40-42] lepers can come to Christ and be miraculously cleansed today.

• If paralytics could rise and be whole at His command in Bible days,[Mk.2:9-12] paralytics can be healed through the power of God's word today.

• If unbelievers could be saved, forgiven of their sins and reborn to a new life then,[Jn.3:3,7; 2Cor.5:17; Eph. 2:8-9; Tit.3:5-6] they can be changed by His power today.

I am glad to have witnessed globally that Jesus Christ is no different in our generation than He was in biblical days.

I have been privileged to have seen Him do thousands of miracles and wonders.

I have been present when He restored paralytics and they walked and ran and jumped.

I have witnessed the marvelous miracle of opening blind eyes hundreds of times.

I have beheld the wonder of Him unstopping deaf ears and loosing dumb tongues.

Jesus said, *All power in heaven and in earth is given to me.*Mat.28:18

His word says, *If we shall ask anything in his name he will do it.*Jn.14:14

The Bible says, *Heaven and earth shall pass away, but my words shall never pass away.*Mat.24:35

We have witnessed the Lord doing these miracles with our own eyes during over a half-century of great gospel crusades in more than a hundred nations. I am convinced that He is unchanged today.

People change. Traditions and religions change. Nations and governments change. Churches and ecclesiastical systems change. But *Jesus Christ is the same yesterday, and today, and forever.*Heb.13:8

The Healing Christ

The Bible says, *Jesus went about all Galilee, teaching in their synagogues, and preaching the gospel of the kingdom, and healing all manner of sickness and all manner of disease among the people.*Mat.4:23

*God anointed Jesus of Nazareth with the Holy Spirit and with power: who went about doing good, and healing all that were oppressed of the devil.*Ac.10:38

The Lord is doing those same miracles of mercy and compassion in this twenty-first century.

A person in the Bible gave a report about one of the meetings where Jesus ministered. He said, *The blind receive their sight, and the lame walk, the lepers are cleansed, and the deaf hear, the dead are raised up, and the poor have the gospel preached to them.*Mat.11:5

Christ did those things then. He does those things today when His promises are believed.

If we want the Lord to do what He did in Bible days, then let us do what people did. Let us come to Him as they came to Him, hear His word as they did, believe on Him, call on Him, and follow Him as the people did then.

The Bible says *they ran through the whole region around about, and began to carry about in beds those that were sick, where they heard he was. And...they laid the sick in the streets, and besought him that they might touch if it were but the border of his garment: and as many as touched him were made whole.*Mk.6:55-56

That takes place today the same as it did then when people put their faith into action. As many as touch Him today are made whole in the same way that people touched Him and were made whole in biblical times.

Death Could Not Stop Him

During three years, Jesus ministered here on earth, healing, blessing and forgiving those who came to Him. Multitudes flocked after Him and He blessed them.Mat.12:15; 14:14; 15:30-31; 19:2; Mk.10:13-16; Jn.6:2

It is astonishing to realize that, despite His mercy, His love and His miracles of compassion, Jesus was despised by religious people, rejected and crucified. Mat.27:26-38; Mk.15:20-38; Lu.23:33-34; Jn.19:16-18

Three days after His interment in a borrowed sepulcher,Lu.23:52-53 God raised Jesus from the dead according to the scriptures.Mat.28:1-6; Lu.24:1-12; Ac.1:2-3;2:32;:13-16; 1Cor.15:4

After His resurrection, Jesus appeared to those who followed Him and commanded them: *Go into all the world and preach the gospel to every creature,* Mk.16:15 [promising that] *whoever believes and is baptized will be saved,* [and warning,] *those who do not believe will be damned.*Mk.16:16

Then He promised: *These signs shall follow them that believe; In my name they shall cast out devils;... they shall lay hands on the sick, and they shall recover.* Mk.16:17-18 *And Lo, I am with you alway, even to the end of the world.*Mat.28:20

That means that the Lord is with me as I write, and that He is with you as you read, wherever you are at this moment.

The Bible says, *So then after the Lord had spoken to them, he was received up into heaven, and sat at the right hand of God. And* [his followers] *went forth, and preached everywhere, the Lord working with them, and confirming the word with signs following.*Mk.16:19-20

The Lord Jesus Christ is with you and me now, to confirm His gospel to us, the same as He was with His disciples after His resurrection. He said, *If you can only believe, all things are possible to those who believe.*Mk.9:23

Whatever He promised in His word, if we earnestly ask Him to do it and if we believe in our heart that He has heard and answered our prayer, He will confirm His promise, and we will receive the blessing for which we have asked.

Christ Has Not Changed

A blind man came to one of our crusades. When he arrived on the grounds, he saw a light that was brighter than the sun, and in that light the Lord Jesus appeared to him. (Paul, in the Bible, had a similar experience.Ac.26:13)

The blind man fell to the ground and the people thought that he died. But after a few moments, he opened his eyes and began to weep as he told them how the Lord had appeared to him. His blindness was gone.

The same Jesus who appeared to that man is with you and me at this moment, to confirm His promises to us, as we believe.

We were preaching in India. A Hindu attended our crusade who was full of animosity. Plotting to disrupt our meeting, he stood at the far edge of the multitude of some 50,000 people, filled with bitterness.

After the message, we prayed for the people. Suddenly Jesus appeared to this man. He stretched out His hands to him and said, *Behold my hands; I am Jesus.*^{Lu.24:39}

When the man saw the nail-pierced hands of the Lord Jesus and looked into His eyes, he fell to the ground, pleading for mercy.^{Jn.20:27-28; Ac.9:4-6; 26: 13-16} He received Jesus Christ into his heart, rushed through the multitude to the platform and urged the people to believe on the Lord.

Jesus Christ has never changed. He is present to confirm His word for us, whether we see Him or not. He says, *If you can only believe, all things are possible.*^{Mk.9:23}

As you hold this book in your hands, draw near to the Lord in your heart. I pray that as you read these pages, Jesus Christ will reveal His truth and manifest His power by whatever miraculous intervention you need in your life today.

He said, *If you shall ask anything in my name, I will do it.*^{Jn.14:14} What do you want Him to do for you at this point in your life?

Believe on the Lord Jesus Christ, and you shall be saved.^{Ac.16:31}

PRAYER BY THE AUTHOR

FATHER IN HEAVEN, I pray for the person who is reading this book. As they ponder the words we have written, let Your presence be manifested in an obvious way. May each chapter be a new and fresh revelation of Your love.

If this reader has not yet been born again, reveal the truth of salvation through this book. If they are suffering sickness or disease, let the biblical truths of Your healing become radiant and clear. Manifest Yourself as the ever-present Healer with whom nothing is impossible.

As these chapters of BIBLICAL HEALING unfold, cause every symptom of disease or sickness or pain to disappear. The Bible says, *You sent your word and healed the people.*[Psa.107:20] You said, *You shall know the truth and the truth shall make you free.*[Jn.8:32] As these chapters are read, may it be a journey of miracles as You confirm each truth presented, proving that You are *the same yesterday, and today, and forever.*[Heb.13:8]

I ask this in the name of Jesus Christ. **AMEN!**

Chapter 2

Miracles—The Biblical Pattern

WHEN JESUS BEGAN His public ministry, it was a ministry of miracles.Mat.4:23-24

His conception, His birth, His life, His wisdom and teaching, His ministry, His death, His resurrection, His appearances, and His ascension were all astounding and undeniable miracles.

When the Church began her ministry, it was a ministry of miracles.Ac.3:1-9; 4:29-30,33

A stream of miracles flowed from the hands of the apostles upsetting religious systems of that day to the extent that even the Roman government trembled.

Those first Christians made the discovery that the Christ whom God raised from the dead had the same power, and worked the same miracles in response to their command—when given in His name—as He had done before He was crucified; that He was alive again; that He lived *in* them; that He had not changed.Ac.3:12-16

The sick were healed.Ac.5:12-16; 8:5-8 The dead were

raised.[Ac.9:36-42; 20:7-12] Demons were cast out in His name.[Ac.16:16-18] Miracles were the hallmark of the ministry of the Early Church.

Christianity—The Miracle Life

Those first years of Early Church history, recorded in the *Acts of the Apostles*, were example years for the *acts of the Church* until the return of Christ—example years of biblical Christianity.

Without the supernatural, Christianity is just a religion, a ritual, a philosophy. *Biblical* Christianity is more than a religion. *It is a Life.*

Religion is a dogma, a creed, a formality, a ceremonial observance.

> *Biblical* Christianity is a *Life*.
>
> It is the living, pulsating heart and nature of Jesus Christ manifested in human persons.

Christianity began in miracles. It is based on a succession of miracles. It is propagated by the miraculous.

The Bible is a miracle book, a record of divine happenings. Beginning with Abraham, many major characters of Old Testament history prayed to God and witnessed miracles in response to their daring and active faith.

The purpose of those miracles was to let the people see the difference between the dead gods of heathendom and the living God who is the Creator of heaven and earth, and to persuade unbelievers to believe and to worship Him.

When miracles ended, the people lapsed into idolatry, and only returned to the living God after another series of miracles.

Humanity wants the living God. They crave a miracle.

Wherever there arises a person whose prayers are heard and answered, greater crowds will flock to hear him or her than to hear the most famous philosopher or statesperson in the world.

Created for Miracles

This love of the miraculous is not a mark of ignorance, but it rather reveals humanity's intense desire to know the unseen God.

In fact, God's purpose and plan for humanity from the beginning, was for people to have supernatural ability and authority. Human beings were created with these aspirations.

Adam and Eve were created in God's image, placed in the garden of Eden, and destined to live and plan and work with God, carrying out His plan on earth.[Gen.1:26-31]

Human persons are God's kind of beings. They

can never be satisfied without Him. They instinctively seek God whether or not they admit it or are conscious of their quest. Human life has divine purpose and until that purpose is discovered, there is a vacuum.

Being the offspring of the miraculous God, people have an innate hunger to experience the miraculous. Education does not eliminate this craving.

Some assert that education has taken the place of miracles; that we no longer need the supernatural to manifest God's existence and love.

But the fact remains that one mighty miracle, wrought in the name of Jesus Christ, accomplishes more to encourage faith in God than a lifetime of theological arguments or philosophical theories.

People want to know if God is real.

• Every spiritual awakening that has honored Christ and His word has been accompanied by the manifestation of the supernatural.

• Wherever and whenever God's word is venerated, the miraculous is evidenced.

• All human persons crave the supernatural. They long to see the power of God exhibited.

• Even an atheistic academician or agnostic professor may edge into the crowd if he or she hears that a miracle may be performed.

• Cultured people will listen to an uneducated preacher if he or she prays and receives answers to their prayers.

This yearning for the miraculous is deep-seated in each human being, regardless of his or her race, color or nationality, because humanity is the offspring of the miracle God.

Men and women need and yearn for the miracle life of Jesus Christ today.

Christ is as much a miracle worker now as He ever was. The Bible says that He *is the same yesterday, and today, and forever.*[Heb.13:8]

Jesus wills to live in us, to manifest His life in and through us. That alone is *biblical* Christianity. All else is ecclesiastical symbolism, rituals, creeds, dogmas, ceremonies.

Jesus attracted the multitudes by miracles,[Mat.12:15; 14:35-36; Lu.5:15; Jn.6:2] and wherever miracles are wrought in His name today, crowds continue to be attracted. We have proven that in nations around the world.

Foundation for Miracles

When anyone exercises biblical faith, biblical results will be experienced.

Why the lack of miracles in many circles today?

The Bible says: *Faith comes by hearing...the word of God.*[Rom.10:17]

But too often, faith may *leave* by hearing the word of theologians who discredit the need and the influence of miracles. Unbelief, instead of faith, is produced when religious leaders *make the word of God of none effect through their tradition.*Mk.7:13

• One may call for a week of fasting, but this will not bring the miraculous into evidence if the promises of God are not taught.

• One may engage in lengthy prayer vigils, but it will be of no avail if simple faith in Christ is not encouraged by teaching His promises.

Both laity and clergy must be willing to adjust their thinking or teaching or actions that do not reflect God's word as being valid today, otherwise, the ministry of BIBLICAL HEALING will not be fostered or experienced.

Religious theology without the supernatural will never produce biblical results. The philosophies of an obsolete ecclesiasticism will never win unbelievers to Christ. To reap the fruit of faith, we must sow the seed of faith. Jesus said, *The seed is the word of God.*Lu.8:11

The sick will be healed and unbelievers will be converted wherever and whenever the gospel of BIBLICAL HEALING is proclaimed and when actions correspond with the teaching.

When Christ's followers *went forth and preached everywhere, the Lord worked with them, confirming the word with signs following.*[Mk.16:15-20] He will always confirm His word whenever it is shared with people by believers.

God *sent his word and* [it] *healed them.*[Psa.107:20] Robert Young's translation says, *He sends his word and heals them.* Like the current of electricity flowing through the wires of one's house, the life of God's word is constantly effective for those who "plug in" to His power by their faith in action.

God's promises are *life to those that find them, and health to all their flesh.*[Prov.4:22]

Ministry of Miracles

Among the tens of thousands who have been miraculously healed by Christ during our own crusades in over a hundred nations, almost none of them have been individually prayed for. They have been healed through their own faith which has been birthed in their own hearts while pondering the biblical truths that we have presented from our crusade platforms, through the pages of our books, or through our audio and video tools.

Jesus warned that religious people sometimes *teach for doctrines the commandments of men and thereby make the word of God of none effect, rejecting the command of God in order to keep their own tradition.*[Mk.7:7-9,13]

Holding to traditions rather than to Christ's promises predominates in many religious circles today. I have discovered that the majority of church members in nations abroad have been well taught in theological *traditions* concerning physical healing. They have been influenced to believe that sickness may be God's blessing in disguise; that it may teach humility and patience; that it may have divine purpose, that it may be God's chastisement, and that, therefore, it should not be resisted but graciously accepted and humbly endured with patience — for God's glory.

But I have also discovered that very few of those people can quote a single biblical verse that promises physical healing.

If the promises of God for BIBLICAL HEALING and miracles are not taught:

- Faith will not be created in the hearts of people.
- The fulfillment of these promises will not be manifested.Rom.10:14; Jn.8:32

If there is no faith for miracles, they will not be experienced.Mat.13:58

The Urgency of Miracles

John said, *a great multitude followed Jesus because they saw his miracles which he did on them that were diseased,*Jn.6:2 [and that] *many believed in his name, when they saw the miracles which he did.*Jn.2:23

When miracles are manifested, unbelievers are drawn to hear the gospel and are persuaded to believe on Christ.

Jesus proclaimed the *gospel of the kingdom of God* Mk.1:14; Mat.9:35 and performed miracles that confirmed the gospel He preached. The Bible says, *He was approved of God by miracles and wonders and signs, which God did by him.* Ac.2:22

Christ's followers in the *Acts of the Apostles* followed His example and the vibrant Early Church prospered as *believers were the more added to the Lord, multitudes both of men and women.* Ac.5:14

Today the need for miracles is as urgent as it was then. Jesus promised, *Believe on me and the works that I do shall you do also; and greater works than these shall you do; because I go to my Father.* Jn.14:12

The key to BIBLICAL HEALING is faith that Christ meant what He said.

It is vital to believe that...

> *God is what He says that He is;*
> *We are what He says that we are;*
> *God has what He says that He has;*
> *We have what He says that we have;*
> *God will do what He says that He will do;*
> *We can do what He says that we can do.*

Whenever and wherever people accept the promises of God and the teachings of Christ, sooner or later spiritual awakenings will take place, accompanied by *signs and wonders and miracles.* Heb.2:3-4

Miracles in this 21st Century are as valuable and as indispensable to biblical Christianity as they ever were in any century.

*I am the Lord, I change not.*Mal.3:6

*Heaven and earth shall pass away, but my words shall never pass away.*Mat.24:35

We have put God's promises to the test in nation after nation. He has proven to be the same in our generation as He was in Bible days.

Jesus—The Miracle Worker

Europe was shocked by the immense crowds and the astonishing miracles which were witnessed by multitudes during our nation-shaking crusade in Holland. It remains the most renowned mass evangelism event in the history of Europe.

Over 100,000 people gathered, day after day, on the great Malieveld grounds in The Hague to listen to the gospel as we presented it to the Hollanders.

Our theme was: *Jesus Christ the same yesterday, and today, and forever.*Heb.13:8 That Bible verse has been emphasized in every crusade we have conducted during more than a half-century of global miracle evangelism ministry.

The people of any nation, deserve to know that Jesus is as real today as He was before He was crucified.

He promised: *Lo, I am with you always.*[Mat.28:20]

He promised: *These signs shall follow them that believe; In my name they shall cast out devils...they shall lay hands on the sick, and they shall recover,*[Mk.16:17-18] [and] *lo, I am with you alway, even to the end of the world.*[Mat.28:20]

Miracles Around the World

In every nation where we have journeyed, great crowds have assembled. Tens of thousands have repented of their sins and have become followers of Jesus Christ. All kinds of miracles have confirmed the gospel that we have proclaimed.

The Bible says the disciples *went forth, and preached everywhere, the Lord working with them, confirming the word with signs following.*[Mk.16:20] This has been our testimony for more than six decades.

God wants us to have confidence in His word and to act upon His promises today. This generation needs miracle proof that Jesus Christ is as real in this century as He was in Bible days.

BIBLICAL HEALING

Part

I

HEALING

❧

THE
BIBLICAL
MANDATE

THE FIRST STEP to receive BIBLICAL HEALING is to know that the age of miracles has not passed, and that physical healing is part of Christ's ministry today.

Chapter 3

Biblical Truths Are For Today

IN BIBLE DAYS, the sick were healed, the blind received their sight, the deaf were made to hear, cripples walked, lepers were cleansed, and all manner of diseased and suffering people were made whole by God's power. These miracles are as much for today as they ever were.

There are five basic reasons why we can know this:

1. GOD is a healer,[Ex.15:26] and He has never changed. *I am the Lord, I change not.*[Mal.3:6]

2. JESUS CHRIST healed the sick,[Mat.9:35; Mk.6:55-56; Ac.10:38] and He has never changed. *Jesus Christ the same yesterday, and today, and forever.*[Heb.13:8]

3. Jesus commanded His DISCIPLES to heal the sick,[Mat.10:1-8; Lu.10:1,8-9] and a true disciple of Christ is the same today. *If you continue in my word, then you are my disciples indeed.*[Jn.8:31]

4. Miracles of healing were manifested in the ministry of the EARLY CHURCH,[Ac.3:6-7; 4:29-30; 5:12; 6:8;8:5-7; 14:3,8-10; 19:11-12; Heb.2:3-4] and the true Church has

never changed. The work and ministry of early Christians is the example and pattern for the biblical Church until *the end of the world.*Mat.28:20

5. Jesus commissioned ALL BELIEVERS, among all nations, until the end of the world, to lay their hands on the sick, promising that *they shall recover,*Mk.16:15-18 and biblical believers have not changed. Jesus said, *Believe on me,* [and] *the works that I do, you shall do also.*Jn.14:12

Miraculous healing was administered:

- First, through the spoken word of Jehovah God;
- Then, through the ministry of the Lord Jesus Christ;
- Next, through His disciples who acted on His word and followed His example;
- Later, through the anointed ministry of the Early Church; and
- Finally, by the power of the Holy Spirit functioning through believers in post-biblical generations.

Therefore, the age of miracles has not passed and physical healing is as much a part of Christ's ministry today as it ever was.

**What He has done
for so many tens of thousands of others,
it is His will to do for you and for me today.**

Chapter 4

100 Facts About
Biblical Healing

MANY PEOPLE BELIEVE that God *sometimes* heals sick people, but they have not known that physical healing is part of God's gift of salvation for *everyone*.

They see other people healed through faith and prayer, but they question whether healing is God's will for them. Meanwhile they may do all that they can to get well through medical science or natural means, whether they think it is God's will for them to be healed or not.

If it is *not* God's will for us to be well, it would be wrong to seek recovery through any means.

If it *is* God's will for us to be well, then the biblical way of recovery through prayer and trust in His promises is the good way for a believer.

The Bible makes the will of God about physical healing as clear as it does about spiritual salvation. When He *promises* to do a thing, it is *His will* to do that thing.

The biblical scriptures conclusively promulgate the fact that God is both *The Savior* and *The Healer* of His people; that it is always His will to *save* and to *heal* those who desire to trust Him.

Here are 100 FACTS
to encourage trust and faith in God for BIBLICAL HEALING:

1. Sickness is no more natural than sin. God made all things *very good.*^{Gen.1:31} Therefore, the best and most thorough remedy for both sin and sickness is to be found in God who created us happy, strong, healthy, and in fellowship with Himself.

2. Both sin and sickness came into the world through the fall of the human race. Therefore, the healing of both is provided in the redemption of humankind.

3. When God sent Moses to lead the children of Israel out of bondage and slavery, He announced His covenant of healing.^{Ex.15:26; 23:25}

Throughout their history, any time they encountered sickness or pestilence, they turned to God in repentance; and always, when their sins were forgiven, their sicknesses were healed.

4. God healed those who were bitten by fiery serpents as they looked at a brazen serpent on a pole, which was a type of Calvary.^{Num.21:8; Jn.3:14-15} If *everyone* who looked at the brazen serpent on the pole was healed then, it is logical that *everyone* who looks to Jesus on the cross can be healed today.

5. Jesus said: *As Moses lifted up the serpent in the wilderness, even so* [for the same purpose] *must the Son of man be lifted up.*Jn.3:14; Num.21:4-9

6. The people had sinned against God then; humankind has sinned against God today.

7. The poisonous serpent's bite resulted in death then; *the wages of sin is death* Rom.6:23 today.

8. The people cried to God then, and He heard their cry and provided a *remedy — the serpent lifted up.* Those who cry to God today discover that He has heard their cry and has provided a remedy — *Christ lifted up.*

9. The remedy was for *everyone bitten* then.Num. 21:8 The remedy is for *whoever believes* today.Jn.3:16

10. In their remedy they received both forgiveness of their sins and healing for their bodies. In Christ, we receive both forgiveness of our sins and healing for our sick bodies today.

11. There were no exceptions then; their remedy was for *everyone bitten.* There are no exceptions today; our remedy is for *whoever believes.*

12. Everyone was commanded to individually look at the remedy then. Everyone is commanded to individually believe on Christ today.

13. They did not need to beg nor make an offering to God then. There was only one condition, *when they look.* We do not need to beg nor make an offering to Christ today. There is only one condition, *whoever believes.*

14. They were not told to look to Moses, but rather to the remedy then. We are not told to look to the preacher, but to Christ today.

15. They were not told to look to the symptoms of their snakebites then, but rather, to *their remedy,* the brazen serpent on a pole. We are not to look to the symptoms of our sins and diseases today, but to *our remedy,* Christ on the cross.

16. *EVERYONE that is bitten, when they look on it, shall live,* was the promise to ALL then, without exception. *WHOEVER believes in him shall not perish, but have everlasting life,*Jn.3:16 is the promise to ALL today, without exception.

17. Since their curse was removed by the lifting up of the "type" of Christ, our curse was removed by Christ Himself being lifted up.Gal.3:13

18. The "type" of Christ could not mean more to those Israelites than Christ Himself means to us today. Surely they, through only a "type" of Christ, could not receive blessings which we cannot receive today through Christ Himself.

19. In Psalm 91, God promises protection for our bodies as well as for our spirits, if we abide in Him. In the New Testament, John wishes *above all things* *that you may prosper and be in health even as your soul prospers.*[3Jo.2] Both scriptures show that God's will is that we be as healthy in our bodies as we are in our spirits.

> **It is never God's will for our spirits to be sick.
> It is never God's will for our bodies to be sick.**

20. Asa died in his sickness, because he sought *NOT to the Lord, but to the physicians.*[2Chr.16:12] Hezekiah lived, because he sought NOT to the physicians, but to the Lord.[Isa.38:1-5] The lesson is not that God is against physicians, but that *HE* must be recognized as our health *source.*

21. The removal of our diseases is included in Christ's redemptive work, along with the removal of our sins. The verbs *borne, carried, took and bare,* [Isa.53: Mat.8:17] imply substitution (suffering *for*), not sympathy (suffering *with*). Since Christ has borne *our* sicknesses and *our* infirmities, obviously we need not bear them again.

22. Christ fulfilled Isaiah's words:[Isa.53:4-5] *He healed all that were sick.*[Mat.8:16-17]

23. The Bible asserts that sickness is from Satan: *Satan went forth...and smote Job with sore boils from the sole of his foot to his crown.*[Job 2:7] Job maintained steadfast faith as he cried out to God for deliverance, and he was healed.[Job 42:10,12]

24. Christ declared that the woman who was bowed over, was bound by Satan and ought to be loosed. He cast out the *spirit of infirmity* Lu.13:11-13,16 and she was healed.

25. A man *possessed with a devil* Mat.12:22 was both blind and dumb. When the devil was cast out, he was healed and could both see and talk.Mat.12:22

26. A lad who was deaf and dumb and who had convulsions, was brought to Jesus for help. When the evil spirit was cast out, the boy was healed. Mk.9:17-27

27. The Bible says, *Jesus of Nazareth...went about ...doing good, and healing ALL that were oppressed of the devil.*Ac.10:38 This Bible verse makes it clear that sickness is Satan's oppression.

28. We are told that *the Son of God was manifested, that he might destroy the works of the devil.*1Jn. 3:8 Sickness is part of Satan's works. Christ, in His earthly ministry, always treated sin, diseases and devils the same; they were all hateful in His sight; He rebuked them all; He was manifested to destroy them all.

29. The Lord does not want the works of the devil to continue in our physical bodies any more than in our spiritual lives. *The Son of God was manifested that he might destroy the works of the devil.*1Jn.3:8

He does not want a cancer, a plague, a curse — *the works of the devil* — to exist in His own members. *Know you not that your bodies are the members of Christ?* 1Cor.6:15

30. Jesus said, *The Son of man is not come to destroy people's lives, but to save them.*Lu.9:56 Sickness destroys life therefore it is not from God. Christ came to save us (Greek: sozo, meaning to deliver us, to save and preserve us, to heal us, to give us life, to make us whole), but never to destroy us.

31. Jesus said, *The thief* [speaking of Satan] *comes to steal, and to kill, and to destroy: I am come that you might have life, and that you might have it more abundantly.*Jn.10:10

32. Satan is a killer; his diseases are the destroyers of life; his sicknesses are the thieves of happiness, health, money, time and effort. Christ came to give us abundant life in our spirits, and physical health in our bodies.

33. We are promised the *life of Jesus in our mortal flesh.*2Cor.4:10-11

34. We are taught that the Spirit's work is to quicken our mortal bodies in this life.Rom.8:11

35. Satan's work is to kill; Christ's work is to give life.

36. Satan is bad. God is good. Bad things come from Satan. Good things come from God.

37. Sickness is, therefore, from Satan. Health is, therefore, from God.

38. All authority and power over all devils and diseases was given to those who followed Christ. Mat.10:1; Mk.16:17-18; Lu.10:19 Jesus said, *If you continue in my word, then are you my disciples indeed.*Jn.8:31 These scriptures apply to you and to me—if we continue in (act on) His word.

39. The Lord has promised every believer that *if you shall ask anything in my name, I will do it.*Jn.14:13-14 This includes asking for healing, if we are sick.

40. *Every one that asks receives.*Mat.7:8 That promise is for every believer, including everyone who may be sick.

41. The ministry of healing was given to the seventy, who represented the future workers of the Church.Lu.10:1,9,19

42. It was given to all *them that believe* Mk.16:17 the gospel; i.e., *them that act* on the gospel, or the *practicers* or *doers* Lu.6:47-48; Rom.2:13; Jas.1:22,25 of the word.

43. It is committed to the elders of the Church. Jas.5:14

44. It is bestowed upon the whole Church as one of its ministries and gifts, until Jesus comes.1Cor.12:9-10

45. Jesus never commissioned anyone to preach the gospel without including healing for the sick. He said: *Into whatever city you enter...heal the sick that are there.*Lu.10:8-9 That command applies to Christian ministry today.

46. Jesus said that He would continue His same works through believers while He is with the Father. He says, *Verily, verily, I say to you, when you believe on me, the works that I do shall you do also; and greater works than these shall you do; because I go to my Father.*[Jn.14:12] That includes healing the sick.

47. In connection with the Lord's Supper, the cup is taken *in remembrance*[1Cor.11:25] of His blood which was shed for the remission of our sins.[Rom. 3:25; Rev.1:5] The bread is eaten *in remembrance* of His body on which were laid our diseases and the stripes by which *we are healed.*[1Cor.11:23-24; Isa.53:5]

48. Jesus said that certain teachers were making *the word of God of none effect through their tradition.*[Mk.7:13] For centuries human ideas and theories have hindered BIBLICAL HEALING from being proclaimed and acted upon, as it was in the Early Church.

49. One tradition is that God wills some of His children to suffer sickness and that, therefore, many who are prayed for are not healed because it is not His will to heal them.

When Jesus healed the demon-possessed boy in Mark, chapter 9, whom the disciples *could not* [Mk. 9:17-18] heal, He proved that it is God's will to heal even those who fail to receive healing. Furthermore, He assigned the failure of the disciples to cure the boy, not to God's will, but to the disciples' *unbelief.* [Mat.17:19-20]

50. The failure of many to be healed today when prayed for is never because it is not God's will to heal them.

51. If sickness is the will of God, then every physician would be a lawbreaker, every trained nurse a defier of the Almighty and every hospital a house of rebellion instead of a house of mercy.

52. Since Christ came to do the Father's will,[Jn. 6:38; Heb.10:7,9] the fact that He *healed them all* is proof that it is God's will that all be healed.

53. If it is not God's will for all to be healed, how did *everyone* in the *multitudes* obtain from Christ the healing that was not God's will for some of them to receive? The Gospel says, *He healed them all.*

54. If it is not God's will for all to be healed, why do the scriptures state: *with his stripes we are healed* [Isa.53:5] [and] *by whose stripes you were healed?* [1Pet.2:24] How could *we* and *you* be declared healed, if it is God's will for some of us to be sick?

55. Christ never refused those who sought His healing. Repeatedly the Gospels tell us that *He healed them all.*[Mat.8:16; 9:35; 12:15; Mk.6:55-56; Lu.4:40; Ac.10:38] Christ the healer has never changed.[Heb.13:8]

56. Only one person in the entire Bible ever asked for healing saying, *If it be your will.*[Mk.1:40] That was the poor leper to whom Jesus immediately responded, *I will; be clean.*[Mk.1:41]

57. Another tradition is that we can glorify God more by being patient in our sickness than by being healed. If sickness glorifies God more than healing, then any attempt to get well by natural or divine means would be an effort to rob God of the glory that we should want Him to receive.

58. If sickness glorifies God, then we should rather be sick than well.

59. If sickness glorifies God, Jesus robbed His Father of all the glory that He could by healing everyone,[Lu.4:40] and the Holy Spirit continued doing the same throughout the life and ministry of the apostles. *They were healed everyone.*[Ac.5:12-16]

60. Paul says, *You are bought with a price; therefore, glorify God in your body, and in your spirit, which are God's.*[1Cor.6:20]

61. Our bodies and our spirits are bought with a price. We are to glorify God in both.

62. We do not glorify God in our *spirit* by remaining in sin; neither do we glorify God in our *body* by remaining sick.

63. The sickness and death of Lazarus are used to prove that sickness glorifies God. But God was not glorified in this case until Lazarus was raised up from the dead, the result of which *many of the Jews...believed on him.*[Jn.11:4,45]

64. Another tradition is that while God heals some, it is not His will to heal all. But Jesus, who came to do the Father's will, did *heal them all.*[Jn.6:38; Mat.8:16; 12:15; Lu.4:40; 6:19]

65. If healing is not for all, why did Jesus bear *our* sicknesses, *our* pains, and *our* diseases? [Isa.53:4; Mat.8:17] If God wanted some of His children to suffer, then Jesus relieved us from bearing something which God wanted us to bear. But since Jesus came to do the *will of the Father,* and since He *has borne our diseases,* it must be God's will for all to be well.

66. If it is not God's will for all to be healed, then God's promises to heal are not for all; that would mean: *Faith* (does not) *come by hearing...the word of God* (alone), but by getting a special revelation that God has favored you and wills to heal you.

67. If God's promises to heal are not for all, then we could not know what God's will is by reading His word alone. That means we would have to pray until He speaks directly to us about each case in particular. We could not consider God's word as directed to us personally, but would have to close our Bibles and pray for a direct revelation from God to know if it is His will to heal each case. That would be absurd. God's word is for all.

68. God's word is His will. God's promises reveal His will. When we read what He promises to do, we then know what is His will to do.

69. Since it is written: *Faith comes by hearing…the word of God,*[Rom.10:17] then the best way to build faith in our hearts that God is willing to heal us, is for us to hear that part of His word that promises healing.

70. Faith for spiritual healing *comes by hearing* the gospel, He *bore our sins.*[1Pet.2:24] Faith for physical healing *sicknesses.*[Mat.8:17]

71. We are to *preach the gospel* [that He bore our *comes by hearing* the gospel, He *bore our* sins] *to every creature.*[Mk.16:15] We are to *preach the gospel* [that He bore our sicknesses] *to every creature.*[Mk.16:15]

72. Christ emphasized His promise, *If you shall ask anything in my name, I will do it,*[Jn.14:13&14] by repeating it twice. He did not exclude healing from this promise. *Anything* includes healing. This promise is for all.

73. If healing is not for all, Christ should have qualified His promise and said, *All things whatever you desire* [except healing], *when you pray, believe that you receive them, and you shall have them.*[Mk.11:24] But He did not. Healing, therefore, is included in the *"whatever."* This promise is made to every person.

74. If it is not God's will to heal all, Christ's promise would not be dependable when He said, *If you abide in me, and my words abide in you, you*

shall ask what you will, and it shall be done to you.
Jn.15:7

75. The Bible says: *Is any sick among you? Call for the elders of the church; and let them pray over the sick, anointing them with oil in the name of the Lord: and the prayer of faith shall save the sick, and the Lord shall raise them up.*Jas.5:14-15 This promise is for all, including you, if you are sick.

76. If God has abandoned healing in answer to prayer today in favor of healing only by medical science, as modern theology speculates, that would mean that He requires us to use a less successful method during a *better* dispensation. *He healed them all* then, but today many diseases are incurable by medical science.

77. Paul tells us that God wants us to be *prepared to every good work,*2Tim.2:21 *thoroughly furnished to all good works,*2Tim.3:17 *that we may abound to every good work.*2Cor.9:8 A sick person cannot measure up to these scriptures. These conditions would be impossible if healing is not for all. Either healing is for all, or these scriptures do not apply to all.

78. Bodily healing in the New Testament was called a *mercy,* and it was God's mercy which always moved Him to heal all the sick. His promise is, *He is plenteous in mercy to all that call upon him.* Psa.86:5 That includes you and me, today.

79. The correct translation of Isaiah 53:4 is: *Surely* [or certainly] *he has borne our sicknesses, and* *carried our pains.* To prove that our sicknesses were carried away by Christ, just like our sins were carried away, the same Hebrew verb for "borne" and "carried" is used to describe both. (See verses 11-12.)

80. Christ was *made to be sin for us* [2Cor.5:21] when *He bore our sins.*[1Pet.2:24] He was *made a curse for us* [Gal. 3:13] when *He bore our diseases.*[Mat.8:17]

81. Since Christ *bore OUR SINS,* how many is it God wills to forgive? Answer: *Whoever believes.* Since Christ *bore OUR sicknesses,* how many is it God wills to heal? Answer: *He healed them all.*

82. Another tradition is that if we are righteous, we should accept sickness as a part of our life. They quote the scripture: *Many are the afflictions of the righteous.*[Psa.34:19] But this does not mean sicknesses as some would have us believe. It means trials, hardships, persecutions, but never sickness or physical disability.

83. It would be a contradiction to say that Christ has borne OUR sicknesses, and with His stripes WE are healed, but then add, *Many are the sicknesses of the righteous* that He requires us to bear.

84. To prove this tradition, theologians quote, *But the God of all grace, who has called us to his eternal glory by Christ Jesus, after that you have suffered a while, make you perfect, establish, strengthen, and settle you.*[1Pet.5:10] This *suffering* does not refer to suffering sickness, but to the many ways in which

God's people have so often suffered for their testimony.Ac.5:41; 7:57-60; 8:12; Col.11:23-27

85. Another tradition is that we are not to expect healing for certain afflictions; the scripture is quoted: *Is any among you afflicted? Let them pray.* Jas.5:13 This again does not refer to sickness, but to the same thing pointed out in numbers 82 and 84 above.

86. Another tradition is that God "chastises" His children with sickness. The scripture in Hebrews 12:6-8 is quoted, a part of which says, *Whom the Lord loves, he chastens.* God does chasten those whom He loves, but the Bible does not say that He imposes physical sickness upon them.

The word "chasten" here means to instruct, train, discipline, teach, or educate, like a teacher instructs a pupil, or like a parent trains and teaches a child.

87. When a teacher instructs a student, various means of discipline are employed but never sickness. When a parent trains a child, different means of punishment are used. But never is physical disease put upon a child by a parent. For our heavenly Father to chastise or punish us does not require that He lay a disease upon us. Our diseases were laid upon Christ. God would not require that we bear, as punishment, what Jesus has borne for us. Christ's sacrifice freed us forever from the curse of sin and disease which He bore for us.

88. The most common tradition is that the age

of miracles is past. For this to be true, there would have to be a total absence of miracles. Even one miracle would prove that the age of miracles is *not* past.

89. If the age of miracles is past, no one could be born again because the NEW BIRTH is the greatest miracle a human person can experience.

90. If the age of miracles is past, as some claim, that would mean that all the technical evidence produced in hundreds of laboratories of the world, concerning innumerable cases of miraculous healings, is false, and that God's promises to do such things are not for today.

91. Anyone who claims that the era of miracles is past denies the need, the privileges and the benefits of prayer. For God to hear and answer prayer, whether the petition is for a postage stamp or for the healing of a cripple, IS A MIRACLE. When prayer brings an answer, it constitutes a miracle.

If there are no miracles, then there is no reason for faith. If there are no miracles, then prayer is fraudulent, and only lack of intelligence could cause a person to pray, expecting an answer.

> **When God answers prayer, that is a miracle.**

Everyone who prays should expect an answer to their prayer. When that prayer is answered, God has performed something beyond the powers of nature or supernatural. That is a miracle. To deny miracles today is to make a mockery of prayer today.

92. The age of miracles is not past, because Jesus, the worker of miracles, has never changed. *Jesus Christ the same yesterday, and today, and for-ever.*Heb.13:8

93. When Jesus sent His disciples to preach the gospel, He told them *These* [supernatural] *signs shall follow them that believe.* Mk.16:17 This was for *every creature,*v.15 for *all nations...until the end of the world.* Mat.28:19-20 The end of the world has not come yet, so the time of miracles has not passed. Christ's Commission has never been withdrawn or annulled.

94. Christ's promise for the spirit, that it shall be *saved*, is in the Great Commission and is for all. His promise for the body, that it shall *recover*, is in His commission and is for all. To deny that one part of Christ's commission is for us today is to deny that the other part is for us today.

As long as the commission of Jesus Christ is in effect, the unsaved can be healed spiritually, and sick people can be healed physically by believing the gospel. Multiplied thousands of sincere people all over the world are receiving the benefits of both physical and spiritual healing through their simple faith in God's promises that they have learned about.

95. Christ bore our sins so that we may be forgiven. Eternal life is ours. As we claim this blessing and confess it by faith, God makes it good in our life.

96. Christ bore our diseases so that we may be healed. Divine health is ours. As we claim this blessing and confess it by faith, God manifests it in our body.

97. Like all of Christ's redemptive gifts, healing must be received by simple faith alone without natural means and, upon being received, must be consecrated for Christ's service and glory alone.

98. God is as willing to heal believers as He is to forgive unbelievers. That is to say, if when we were unsaved, God was willing to forgive us, now that we are His child, He is willing to heal us. If He was merciful enough to forgive us when we were unconverted, He is merciful enough to heal us now that we are members of His royal family.[Rom.8:32]

99. We must accept God's promise as true and believe that we are forgiven before we can experience the joy of spiritual healing. We must accept God's promise as true and believe that we are healed before we can experience the joy of physical healing.

100. *As many* [sinners] *as received him...were born ...of God.*[Jn.1:12-13] *As many* [sick] *as touched him were made whole.*[Mk.6:56]

When we preach that it is always God's will to heal, the question is often raised: How then would we ever die?

The Bible says: *He takes away their breath, they die, and return to the dust.*[Psa.104:29] *You shall come to your grave in a full age, like as a shock of corn comes in its season.*[Job 5:26]

For us to come to our full age and for God to take away our breath does not require the aid of a disease. God's will for our death as His child is that, after living a fruitful life, *fulfilling the number of our days,*[Ex.23:25-26] we simply stop breathing and fall asleep in Christ, to awaken with Him and to live with Him forever. *So shall we ever be with the Lord.*[1Th.4:17] This is the blessed hope of the righteous.[1Th.4:13; Tit.2:13; 1Pet.1:3]

Because they [the righteous] *have set their love upon me,* [God says], *therefore will I deliver them: I will set them on high, because they have known my name. They shall call upon me, and I will answer them: I will be with them in trouble; I will deliver them, and honor them. With long life will I satisfy them, and show them my salvation.*[Psa.91:14-16]

ACKNOWLEDGMENT: *In presenting these 100 facts about* BIBLICAL HEALING, *I am indebted to the resourceful writings of my intimate friend and mentor, F.F. Bosworth, from which many of the thoughts expressed here have been gleaned.*

Part

II

SCRIPTURE

❧

THE
HEALING
AUTHORITY

THE SECOND STEP to receive BIBLICAL HEALING is to know God's promises to heal, in the scriptures, and to be convinced that they are for *you* personally.

Chapter 5

God Speaks
Through His Word

RELIGIOUS TEACHERS often do us more harm than good by making a philosophy or a doctrine out of biblical truth, when it is meant to be as though the Lord is speaking to us. The word of God is His voice to us. It has His same authority.

• When we read the Bible, the Lord is speaking to us personally.

• The integrity of God's written word is the only trustworthy basis for biblical faith.

One of the greatest spiritual errors is treating the word of God as though it were an ordinary book. We learn to give it the same place we would give Christ if He were physically in our presence. His word speaks to us, and tells us the same things that He would say if He spoke to us audibly.

We do not separate God from His word.

He is not only in it — a part of it — but He is back of it, continually *watching over it to confirm it.*^{Jer.1:12;}

Isa.55:11; Mat.24:35 To assure that, as Solomon said, *there has not failed one word of all his good promises, which he promised.*1Kg.8:56 The angel said: *No word from God is void of power.*Lu.1:37RV Another translation says, *No promise from God will be impossible of fulfillment.*

He Is Speaking to Us

An old man lay dying in his shack . A Christian woman read to him: *For God so loved the world, that he gave his only begotten Son, that whoever believes in him should not perish, but have everlasting life.*Jn.3:16

The old man opened his eyes and looked at the lady asking, "Is that in the Bible?"

"Yes," she said.

"Does it mean me?"

"Certainly it means you," she assured him.

He pondered her words for a few moments, then asked, "Has God said anything else to me in that book?"

Then she read: *As many as received him, to them gave he power to become the children of God.*Jn.1:12 Then she added softly, "He is speaking to you."

The old man opened his eyes and whispered, "I believe that. I accept Him. I am satisfied." Then he died.

He treated God's written word as though Jesus Christ had visited him in person and had brought him the message of eternal life.

The promises that we read in the Bible are God speaking to us personally. They are just as much ours as a check that is payable to our name. We cash that check because it is ours. In the same way, we claim God's promises in prayer because they are ours.

Knowing that physical healing is a part of Christ's ministry today, we know that His promises to heal, in the Bible, are for us personally.

God's Word Speaks To Us

A man who had been deaf in one ear for twenty years, came to me for prayer. I asked him if he believed that God would heal his ear. He replied: "I don't know. I hope so—if it is His will."

"Are you aware that God has *promised* to heal you?" I asked him.

"No," he replied, "I didn't know that."

"Do you believe that God is good enough to do something if He promised to do it?"

"Yes sir, I do," he answered without hesitation, then added, "I do that when I make a promise."

"If I can show you in the Bible that God has promised to heal *you*, do you believe that He will do it?" I asked.

"Yes," he replied, "I believe He would *if He promised to.*"

I looked right into his eyes and quoted these biblical verses, then posed a question after each one.

1. *I am the Lord that heals you.*Ex.15:26
   Who does **you** mean?

2. *By whose stripes you were healed.*1Pet.2:24
   Who does **you** mean?

3. *Who heals all your diseases.*Psa.103:3
   Who does **your** mean?

The man began to weep and responded, "I didn't know that God had promised to heal *me*. I understand now, and I believe that He will do it."

Faith came to that man by hearing God's promises. Paul said, *Faith comes by hearing...the word of God.*Rom.10:17

I touched his ear in Jesus' name, asking God to open it according to His promise, and it was immediately healed.

God's promises are just as much for you and for me as they were for that man.

If you shall ask anything in my name, I will do it. Jn.14:14 *Anything* includes healing.

*Is any sick among you?...the prayer of faith shall save the sick and the Lord shall raise him up.*Jas.5:14-15 *Any* includes you and me. The promise, *the Lord shall raise him up*, is made without exception.

*These signs shall follow them that believe...they shall lay hands on the sick, and they shall recover.*Mk.16:17-18

This is for you and for me, if we *believe. They shall recover* is Christ's promise to everyone who is sick, without exception.

Faith means that we believe God's promises are for us. We claim them in sincere prayer, and God fulfills them. We have no reason to doubt. We believe His word as though He were speaking to us personally.

Chapter 6

Why Healing
Is For Today

GOD ANNOUNCES: *I am the Lord who heals you.*
Ex.15:26

He is *The Healer*. It is His will to heal us.

It may be difficult for some people to reconcile this statement with so much sickness and disease in our world.

It may also seem awkward to harmonize this truth with traditional religious teaching about physical sickness.

But when we comprehend that God's word of promise is addressed to us personally, we become aware that His will is for us to enjoy physical health, spiritual salvation and material abundance.

No scripture could express God's will more clearly than this one:

> *I wish above all things that you may prosper and be in health, even as your soul prospers.*3Jn.2

The Bible teaches that when Jesus Christ died on the cross, He *bore* our physical infirmities, diseases and pains in the same way that He *bore* our sins and our iniquities.

Our Substitute

The question is not: Did He bear our physical diseases?

The question is: Why did He bear them?

The same verbs (in both Hebrew and Greek) used to state that He *bore* our spiritual iniquities is used to state that He *bore* our physical diseases.[Isa. 53:4-5; Mat. 8:16-17; 1Pet.2:24]

Why did He bear our physical diseases in the same way that He bore our sins?

The answer constitutes the essence of the Good News — good news for those who are sick as well as for those who have not been converted.

- He did it so that we do not have to do it.

- He did it as our personal substitute.

- This is what *redemption* is all about.

- This is why you and I can be healed.

Chapter 7

Biblical Healing
For Everyone

THE LIFE OF CHRIST includes physical health for you and for me.

It is God's will for us to be physically healed as well as to be spiritually saved.

> *Who forgives all your iniquities;*
> *who heals all your diseases.*Psa.103:3

Healing and forgiveness are gifts of God which are to be received by faith.

Faith is expecting God to do what He promised to do. That is why *faith comes by hearing...the word of God.*Rom.10:17

God has given to us His promises 2Pet.1:4 in order to reveal to us His will.

His *testament,* His *will,* His *promise* and His *word* are the same.

In order to receive blessings from God, they are

to be embraced with childlike faith. To have faith for any blessing, we must first be convinced that such a blessing is God's will for us. As long as we question whether or not God wills that we receive something, we will not appropriate it by faith.

His Promise Is His Will

The Bible teaches us to ask for blessings, believing that we receive them. *Ask in faith, nothing wavering. For the person who wavers is like a wave of the sea driven with the wind and tossed. Let not that person think that he or she will receive anything of the Lord.*Jas.1:6-7

Anyone can be saved when he or she believes that Christ died for their sins. Because of His sacrifice to redeem them, they can know that it is God's will and desire to forgive them. They accept God's gift of new life by faith and are born again. Salvation is for *whoever will.*Jn.3:16

In the same way, a person can be healed when he or she believes that Christ bore their sicknesses and diseases. Because of His sacrifice to provide healing for them, they can know that it is God's will and desire to physically heal them and they are made whole. BIBLICAL HEALING is for *everyone.*

If we are sick, we read the Bible and become convinced by God's promises that it is His will to heal us physically. Otherwise, we are not able to ask for healing with confidence that it will be received.

Religious tradition teaches that one should ask for healing by praying, *if it be God's will*. But this uncertainty implies questioning the veracity of God's promises to heal. Those who pray for physical healing using the faith-destroying phrase, "If it be Thy will," do not usually receive the answer because they have not asked in faith.

No biblical believer would tell a person seeking salvation to pray for God to save them "if it is His will." His promise to save *whosoever believes* proves His will to save all who call on Him.

God has abundantly promised to heal those who believe. (My book, HEALING THE SICK—called *A Living Classic* by the publisher, has been acclaimed worldwide as one of the greatest faith-builders for physical healing in print.) *www.osborn.org*

God Wills to Heal All

The purpose of this chapter is to emphasize that God's will is to heal *everyone* who has faith in His promises. According to the Bible, His *salvation* includes physical health for God's glory.

Soon after Christ was raised from the dead, His followers put His words into practice. The biblical record of their ministry illustrated God's will in action wherever the gospel was proclaimed.

By the hands of the apostles were many signs and wonders wrought among the people.

And believers were the more added to the Lord, multitudes both of men and women:

Insomuch that they brought forth the sick into the streets, and laid them on beds and couches...

There came also a multitude out of the cities round about to Jerusalem, bringing sick folks, and them which were vexed with unclean spirits: and they were healed EVERY ONE.[Ac.5:12-16]

These words, ***they were healed every one***, reveal what God's will is today for all who are sick.

This is a record of what was accomplished under Peter's ministry in Jerusalem *after* Jesus had returned to the Father.

It was a testimony that Christ's ministry did not change after His ascension.

They were healed every one was a fulfillment of God's healing covenant, *I am the Lord that healeth thee.*[Ex.15:26]

• *"Thee"* in that covenant included *"every one"* in Jerusalem under Peter's ministry, and it includes both you and me today.

• *They were healed every one* was experienced by the entire nation of Israel—nearly three *million* people.[Num.1:45-46] *There was not ONE FEEBLE PERSON among their tribes.*[Psa.105:37]

• *They were healed every one* was experienced by each sick person amidst the throngs that followed

Jesus: *Great multitudes followed him, and he healed them all.*[Mat.12:15]

• *They were healed every one* is what happened to *"every one"* of the Israelites in the wilderness who were bitten by fiery serpents: When they *beheld the serpent of brass* lifted up on a pole, [a type of Calvary][Jn.3:14-15] *THEY lived*[Num.21: 8-9] – *all* of them.

• *They were healed every one* is what happened when *God sent his word and healed them.*[Psa.107:20] That is the purpose of His word concerning BIBLICAL HEALING for you and for me today; so that *every one* can be healed.

• *They were healed every one* is God's will for today. It includes both you and me. It will save us from premature death: *I will take sickness away from the midst of you…the number of your days I will fulfill.*[Ex.23:25-26]

No Exceptions

To make it possible for *every one* to be healed, *Christ has redeemed us from the curse of the law.*[Gal.3:13] This *curse* includes *every sickness and every plague.* [Deut.28:61] *"Us"* includes *every one.*

• This blessing was provided for *every one* at Calvary when *certainly he suffered our pains and carried our diseases.*[Isa.53:4LT] *"Our"* includes *every one.*

• This was made possible because *with his stripes we are healed.*[Isa.53:5; 1Pet.2:24] *"We"* includes *every one.*

• This was made possible when *Himself took our infirmities, and bare our sicknesses.*Mat.8:17 *"Our"* includes *every one.*

• When Christ *came down from heaven, not to do* [His] *own will, but the will of him that sent* [Him],Jn.6:38 He repeatedly *healed them all.*Mat.12:15; 14:36; Lu.6:19; Ac.10:38 His own ministry on earth demonstrated His will to heal everyone.

• *They were healed every one* was the standard in Christ's ministry. It was what He promised to the believers. *When you believe on me, the works that I do shall you do also.*Jn.14:12

• *They were healed every one* was what *Jesus began both to do and teach, until the day in which he was taken up,*Ac.1:1-2 and then continued to do after He was taken up and seated at the Father's right hand. Ac.5:16; 28:9

• *They were healed every one* is the will of God now while Christ is seated in heaven: *Jesus Christ the same yesterday, and today, and forever.*Heb. 13:8

• *They were healed every one* is as much the will of God as it is His will to forgive every sinner who repents. *Who forgives all…who heals all.*Psa.103:3

• *They were healed every one.* This blessing is for every city: *Into whatever city you enter…heal the sick that are there.*Lu.10:8-9 "The sick" includes everyone who is physically ill.

• *They were healed every one* attracts people to hear the gospel, including those from surrounding towns and cities. *There came also a multitude out of the cities round about unto Jerusalem.*[Ac.5:16]

• *They were healed every one* results in *multitudes both of men and women* [being] *added to the Lord.*[Ac.5:14] The first healing miracle in Acts caused *about five thousand people* [to] *believe on Christ.*[Ac.4:4]

• *They were healed every one* is one of the ways in which God *bore witness to this great salvation both with signs and wonders and with divers miracles, and gifts of the Holy Ghost.*[Heb.2:3-4]

This is the ministry which has caused multiplied thousands of *non*-Christians to believe the gospel in our own crusades globally.

Healing in the Bible

• *They were healed every one.* The Early Church prayed for this before the sick were brought from the surrounding areas to the streets of Jerusalem for healing. They prayed for the Lord to *stretch forth His hand to heal and to do signs and wonders by the name of Jesus.*[Ac.4:30]

• *They were healed every one.* Even the physically well and strong united to bring about this result. *They* brought *the sick into the streets, and laid them on beds and couches.*[Ac.5:15]

• *They were healed every one.* This is what the whole Church is to pray for *in one accord,* as the

Early Church did: *They lifted up their voice to God with one accord.*Ac.4:24

• *They were healed every one.* This was accomplished for all when the sick did not get as close to Peter as the people got to Jesus when *they laid the sick in the streets, and begged him to let them touch the border of his garment: and as many as* **touched** *him were made whole.*Mk.6:56 They did not even touch Peter. Only *his shadow passed over some of them,* yet *they were healed every one* and there were *multitudes* of them.

• *They were healed every one.* This is the result the Holy Spirit longs to accomplish everywhere: a) He interceded for it,Ac.4:24-30 b) He accomplished it, Ac.5:12-16 and c) He recorded it so that every creature could hear and read about it, and thus have faith for it to be repeated today.

For *All* Then—For *All* Now

• *They were healed every one* would have included you, had you been sick and present there that day. Healing, therefore, is for you today because God's will, which was executed in Jerusalem, has never changed.

• *They were healed every one* included all of *them which were vexed with unclean spirits.*Ac.5:16 The demon-possessed are included in God's will for healing today.

• *They were healed every one.* This can be the same

today when everyone believes the truth about healing. Jesus said: *You shall know the truth, and the truth shall make you free.*[Jn.8:32]

• *They were healed every one.* This is included in Christ's promise: *Anyone who comes to me, I will not cast him or her out.*[Jn.6:37] Every sick person in Jerusalem, from the cities round about Jerusalem,[Ac.5: 15-16] and in the *villages, cities and country*[Mk.6:56] proved that this blessing was for them.

• *They were healed every one.* This blessing is for you and for me. Christ says: *According to your faith be it done to you.*[Mat.9:29] He promises, *when you pray, believe that you receive* [the things you ask for], *and you shall have them.*[Mk.11:24]

• *They were healed every one.* This is God's will today. It is His will for you and for me—now. He promises, *everyone that asks receives.*[Mat.7:8]

Chapter 8

Healing Is
Spiritual And Physical

THIS MESSAGE OF good news (the gospel) *is the power of God unto salvation to every one that believes.*[Rom.1:16] That includes you and me today.

I cannot explain how Jesus suffered our diseases and our pains on the cross so many years ago. It is not logical or reasonable. Perhaps this is why *the preaching of the cross is to them that perish foolishness; but unto us which are saved it is the power of God.*[1Cor.1:18]

But when we *believe in our heart and confess with our mouth* [Rom.10:9-10] what the Bible says that Jesus did for us on the cross, then God confirms it by His miracle power. Jesus said, *Only believe.*[Mk.5:36]

Christ paid for our perfect and complete healing when He died in our place. He is the Lord *Who heals all our diseases.*[Psa.103:3] He paid for our healing when He *carried our diseases and suffered our pains, taking the stripes by which we were healed.*[Isa.53: 4-5]

It is finished[Jn.19:30] now. Our health is paid for.

Our diseases were laid upon Him.[Mat.8:17] He took them away forever. Healing belongs to us now. It is God's gift to us. It belongs to us. Satan has no right to lay on us what God laid on Jesus.

What Christ Bore, We Need Never Bear

The Lord has laid on him the iniquity of us all.[Isa.53:6]

For the transgression of my people was he stricken.[Isa.53:8]

It pleased the Lord to bruise him…[and to make] his soul an offering for sin.[Isa.53:10]

For he shall bear their iniquities.[Isa.53:11]

He bore the sins of many.[Heb.9:28]

He was wounded for our transgressions, he was bruised for our iniquities: the chastisement of our peace was upon him.[Isa.53:5]

Certainly he has borne our sicknesses and carried our pains.[Isa.53:4LT] *With his stripes we are healed.*[Isa.53:5]

Himself took our infirmities, and bare our sicknesses. [Mat.8:17] Why? So that we do not have to bear them; so that we can be healed and enjoy health and happiness.

Who his own self bore our sins in his own body on the tree. [Why?] That we, being dead to sins, should live unto righteousness.[1Pet.2:24]

What is the result of this freedom from sin and

evil? *By whose stripes you were healed,*[1Pet.2:24] spiritually, mentally and physically.

When sin entered the human family, sickness followed. The devastation of deceit and evil, the decadence of lust and envy, the deadly destructive influence of hatred and vengeance, the corruption of sin and rebellion all impose their destructive toll on the human body. It is poisoned by the noxious effect of attitudes that are negative and depraved.

Salvation and healing are free gifts of God to rescue and to heal humanity, not only from the evil of sin, but from its terrifying physical effects upon the human body.

Who his own self bore our own sins in his own body on the tree, [so that we may be saved and] *live unto righteousness.*[1Pet.2:24]

Himself took our infirmities, and bare our sicknesses,[Mat.8:17] so that we may be healed and made whole.

Forgiveness of sins and physical healing are part of the *great salvation*[Heb.2:3] which we are told not to neglect. Both spiritual and physical healing are provided for us. Salvation includes both. The spirit and the body both need healing. Jesus always healed both.

Physical and Spiritual Healing

Who forgiveth all thine iniquities; who healeth all thy diseases.[Psa.103:3]

Which is easier to say, your sins be forgiven you; or to say, Arise, and walk? Mat.9:5

For this people's heart is waxed gross, and their ears are dull of hearing, and their eyes have been closed; lest at any time they should see with their eyes, and hear with their ears, and should understand with their heart, and should be converted and I should heal them. Mat.13:15

Are any sick among you?...the prayer of faith shall save the sick, and the Lord shall raise them up; and if they have committed sins, they shall be forgiven them. Jas.5:14-15

The healing that God offers through the cross of Christ is total health for the total person—spiritual, mental and physical—and that health is for you and it is for me today.

Part
III

SATAN

❧

THE
DISEASE
SOURCE

> **T**HE THIRD STEP to receive BIBLICAL HEALING is to understand that God wants you to be well; that only Satan wants you to suffer.

Chapter 9

The Root
Of Sickness

THE FAITH OF MANY who seek healing from Christ is hindered by the idea that God may have permitted their sickness, or even placed it upon them, for some purpose, and that they should have patience and not seek physical healing through prayer and faith in His promises. Thousands of people suffer needlessly for years, and die prematurely because of these and other concepts presumed by church tradition.

To avoid these mistaken theories, we need to remember that sickness and disease are *destructive* and that they therefore emanate from *the destroyer,* Satan, and not from God. Jesus said, *the thief* [Satan] *cometh not, but to steal, and to kill, and to* **destroy.** Jn.10:10

I was active in gospel ministry for seven years before I heard a minister say that the source of sickness is our enemy — the killer — Satan.

This idea astounded me at first because I assumed that sickness and disease were a normal part of life. I had never thought of them as being influences of *death* at work in the human body. I began to search the scriptures about this and discovered information I had not observed.

Satan's Part in Disease

The biblical case of Job first alerted me: *Satan went forth...and smote Job with sore boils.*[Job2:7] Satan was the source of his sickness.

Then I noted that Jesus said of a woman who *was bowed together, and could in no wise lift up herself,* [that] *Satan has bound her;* [that she had a] *spirit of infirmity.*[Lu.13:11-16]

I read about a man who was *possessed with a devil, blind and dumb.* [When Jesus cast out the devil], *the blind and dumb both spake and saw.*[Mat.12:22]

I found another case where a *foul spirit* caused a lad to have convulsions and to be deaf and dumb. When the *deaf and dumb spirit* was cast out by Jesus, the lad was perfectly whole.[Mk.9:25-27]

I was profoundly impressed by the Bible verse that says, *Jesus went about...healing all that were oppressed of the devil.*[Ac.10:38] This affirms that all the sick people whom Christ healed were considered to be *oppressed of the devil.* The Early Church identified sickness as Satan's *oppression.*

I heard a Bible teacher explain something about healing that I had never heard before. It helped me to understand the ministry of healing and my life and ministry were changed as a result. He explained Satan's part in disease as follows:

Spirit of Infirmity

"Every disease has a life, a germ. Because it is destructive, the source of that germ is Satan, *the destroyer*. [Jn.10:10] Jesus called it a *spirit of infirmity*. [Lu.13:11-13] That germ causes disease to grow in the same way that the germ of life at our conception has caused us to grow as a human body. When that germ, or life, leaves our body, it will die, decay and return to the dust. When the spirit of a disease leaves, the physical disease dies, decays and disappears."

This minister explained further: "Those who have received Christ by faith and have become part of God's family, have authority over the spirits of the devil. [Lu.9:1-2,6; 10:1,8-9,19] He quoted Jesus: *In my name you shall cast out devils*. [Mk.16:17] Clearly, believers are authorized to command the destructive life of disease to leave the body of one who trusts in Christ. When it leaves, the disease dies and the effects of it disappear."

Then, the Bible teacher illustrated his point:

"For example, a cancer or growth or disease has a life in it. The source of that destructive life is *the* destroyer – the killer – Satan.[Jn.10:10] As long as the life of disease exists in the infirmity, it will continue its deadly work. When the life or *spirit* of the cancer or disease is commanded to leave, in Jesus' name, the sickness dies, decays, dissolves and from that moment, disappears. The person *recovers*."[Mk.16:18]

Our Lives Were Changed

My attitude toward BIBLICAL HEALING by faith in Christ was reformed. I realized that, as a Bible believer, I was authorized by my Lord to pray for sick people [Jn.14:12-14] and, for the first time, I had reason to expect them to recover.

I had been given authority, in Jesus' name, to rebuke the *spirits of infirmity* that cause disease and to command them to leave. The sicknesses would die and the sufferers would recover. Jesus *gave* [us] *power and authority over all devils, and to cure diseases.*[Lu.9:1] He said, *In my name they shall cast out devils…they shall lay hands on the sick, and they shall recover.*[Mk.16:17-18]

We began inviting sick people to our meetings. We instructed them thoroughly in the words and promises of Jesus Christ, which is of prime importance if we expect them to be healed. Then, we prayed for those who were sick, rebuking the spirits of infirmities and commanding them to leave in Jesus' name. The diseases died, and the sick people recovered according to the Lord's promise.[Mk.16:18]

Christ confirmed His word and God was glorified not only in the healing of the sick, but in the salvation of so many souls. Often we have led more people to Christ in one day by including the healing part of the gospel in our message, than we did in seven years combined, before we proclaimed Christ as healer.

We rebuked the blind spirit which had caused a cataract on a man's eye. The blind spirit left, the cataract died and in a few days, the cataract dissipated and his sight was restored.

We rebuked the spirit which had caused a man to be deaf, commanding it to leave in Jesus' name. His hearing became normal.

We commanded the life of a cancer to leave a woman. The cancer died, and the sick woman recovered.

People who had suffered all kinds of diseases recovered according to Christ's promise. We soon began hearing reports: "I was prayed for and now I am healed." "I had a tumor and now it is gone." "The cancer has disappeared from my body."

New faith was evidenced in our church and its influence spread throughout the area. We had taken the Bible promises seriously and were ministering BIBLICAL HEALING to the whole person. *Christ was working with us, confirming his word with signs following.*[Mk.16:20]

This has been our life's work for over sixty years

and it is what we continue to do throughout the world. With the authority that the Lord has given us over devils and diseases, we rebuke the *spirits of infirmities* which cause illnesses, commanding them to leave the bodies of the sick. The people recover and thousands of souls accept the gospel and receive Christ as savior in every mass miracle gospel crusade that we conduct.

The miraculous power of Christ, when manifested today, in the healing of sick people, influences thousands of souls to believe on Christ as savior, as it did in Bible days.

*Many believed in his name, when they saw the miracles which he did.*Jn.2:23

And a great multitude followed him, because they saw his miracles which he did on them that were diseased. Jn.6:2

*Then...when they had seen the miracle that Jesus did, said, This is of a truth that prophet that should come into the world.*Jn.6:14

*Believers were added to the Lord, multitudes both of men and women.*Ac.5:14 This happened when *they brought the sick into the streets, and laid them on beds and couches...and they were healed every one.*Ac.5:15-16

As long as a person thinks that their sickness or disease may be from God, or that He may have some mysterious purpose in the infirmity, they will not resist it's deadly influence.

But when one understands what the Bible clearly teaches, that the source of disease is Satan—the

Killer — the Destroyer, that person will resist sickness as an enemy, will rebuke it, refuse it, and as they trust in Christ's Life at work within them, the deadly spirit of infirmity will leave them and they will recover from their illness.

The Source of Sickness

Medical personnel may call a disease that stiffens the joints "arthritis" or "rheumatism." But in biblical terms, the cause is the *oppression of the devil*.[Ac.10:38] Deafness may be called "deadened ear nerves," but biblically, the source is a spirit of deafness.

A technician might diagnose a lad who cannot speak as having "undeveloped vocal cords," but the biblical term is a dumb spirit.

The specialist may call blindness "glaucoma" or "cataracts," but in biblical terms, it is a blind spirit.

A blind woman was brought to us for prayer. Optometrists said her optical nerves were dead. From a medical standpoint their analysis was correct but in biblical terms, a blind spirit was the cause. For fifteen years she had been guided by a seeing-eye dog.

In Jesus Christ's name we rebuked the spirit of blindness which had destroyed her sight. It left her and the lady screamed with joy, "Now I can see! I am healed!" Her sight was restored.

A woman was brought to our crusade, transported in a wheelbarrow by three women friends. She had suffered a radical stroke of paralysis.

For four days and nights she had not swallowed water or food. Her eyes did not focus and her body appeared to be dead, except for the irregular pulse of her heart.

We rebuked the spirit of infirmity, commanding it to leave. Then I called: "Veda, open your eyes and be healed in Jesus' name." She was restored within a few minutes, and was able to walk home, sound and well.

The cause of her illness was a *spirit of infirmity* which had been sent by Satan to destroy her life. Jn.10:10 But God healed her.

Jesus said: *Have faith in God.*Mk.11:22

When we understand that Satan is the deadly source of disease and that a *spirit of infirmity* is the life of the sickness, then we can calmly rebuke the disease in Jesus' name, commanding the *spirit of infirmity* to leave, and we can be sure that the illness is dead and will dissipate.

> **God who is good — God, *the Life giver* wants people to be well.**
>
> **Only Satan, the destroyer — the thief — the killer, wants human persons to suffer disease.**

Chapter 10

God's Plan
Contaminated By Sin

GOD CREATED Adam and Eve perfect physically, mentally, spiritually, and He placed them in the Garden of Eden, a place of happiness, tranquility and abundance. That was His plan for you and for me.

1. He warned them: *Of every tree of the garden thou mayest freely eat: But of the tree of the knowledge of good and evil, thou shalt **not** eat of it; for in the day that thou eatest thereof **thou shalt surely die**.*Gen.2:17

2. But Satan persuaded them to doubt God's word suggesting: *Hath God said, Ye shall **not** eat of every tree of the garden?*Gen.3:1 Then he added his lying contradiction: *Ye shall **not surely die**.*Gen.3:4

3. The result: *When the woman saw that the tree was good for food, and that it was pleasant to the eyes, and a tree to be desired to make one wise, she took of the fruit thereof, and did eat, and gave also unto her husband with her; and he did eat.*Gen.3:6

That was sin, and sin brought shame.[Gen.3:8-10] They had disobeyed God's word, and were consequently separated from the paradise which God had created for them to enjoy.[Gen.3:23-24]

They became slaves of Satan. All that was perfect began to deteriorate. Happiness turned to sadness, love to hatred. Life was plagued by disease and eventual death. Beauty faded. Faith turned to distrust, and confidence to deception.

The healthy bodies that God had created became subject to the deterioration of disease and pain—subject to Satan's purpose which is *to steal, and to kill, and to destroy.*[Jn.10:10]

Suffering and sickness, deterioration and infirmity became the incurable curse that ravaged humanity until the only relief from this torture chamber was death itself—the final blow to God's human creation.

Sin and sickness have plagued humanity throughout all generations since Adam and Eve. Physical beauty and health have been scarred by every imaginable form of disease. The human mind and spirit have become poisoned by the influences of sin and corruption.

Despite the triumphs of medical science, human beings are still menaced by psychological and physical deterioration and disease.

Chapter II

Health Replaced
By Disease

IT WAS NEVER God's plan for humankind, whom He created in perfection, to suffer mental or physical diseases.

The problem of sickness and physical weakness began when Adam and Eve yielded to Satan's temptation to question God's word. Sin was conceived and *sin, when it is finished, bringeth forth death.*[Jas.1:15] They were separated from His presence. The seeds of sin grew and produced inevitable death in the lives of hurting humanity.

God saw that wickedness was great in the earth, and that every imagination of the thoughts of the heart was only evil continually...and it grieved him.[Gen.6:5-6]

Disharmony and deceit, jealousy and hatred, envy and lust, violence and murder disrupted the entire structure of the human person.

This discord produced an ever-growing, menacing harvest of physical pain, suffering, disease and deterioration.

Deuteronomy, chapter 28, outlines the deadly penalty and curse of disobedience to God. It enumerates a list of specific physical diseases which people suffer.[Deut.28:15,20-22,27-29,35,60-67] Then a comprehensive footnote is added to the ominous catalog: *Also every sickness, and every plague, which is not written in the book of this law.*[Deut.28:61]

But God, who is love—God who created man and woman *in his own image,*[Gen.1:26-27] could not abandon His dream. At the very time they were rebelling against Him, being separated from His presence, sinking into depravation and despair, His immense love was impelling Him to find a way to buy back (or to redeem) His creation from Satan who had defrauded and enslaved them.

God's own law made it clear that whoever sinned must be punished. *The soul that sins shall die.*[Eze.18:4,20] *The wages of sin is death.*[Rom.6:23] *But all had sinned,*[Rom.5:12] so all must suffer and die.

Only an innocent, sinless *One* could become a substitute for the guilty. Therefore, God loved us so much that He gave His only Son as our ransom.[1Tim.2:5-6; Mk.10:45] Jesus Christ, the innocent One, suffered the penalty and endured the punishment that guilty humanity deserved.

Chapter 12

Sin's Penalty Is Paid

THE GOSPEL is good news. What good news?

It is the Good News of what Jesus accomplished for you and for me through the sacrifice of His life. On the cross, He endured the punishment for our sins. Why? So that we do not need to be punished.

The 53rd chapter of Isaiah which is a prophecy of the redemption of humanity by Christ says: *Certainly he has borne our sicknesses and carried our pains.*[Literal Hebrew] When He suffered our penalty on the cross, Isaiah said the people thought that Jesus was being punished by God.[Isa.53:4]

But, the redemptive fact is that *He was wounded for our transgressions, he was bruised for our iniquities: the chastisement of our peace was upon him; and with his stripes we are healed.*[Isa.53:5]

If He suffered our diseases and bare our pains, then, logically, *we are healed.* This is the same as to say: "My friend paid my debts, and by his paying them in my name, I am debt-free."

A debt does not exist, once it has been paid. It is absolved, expunged. One has no more obligation. The same debt cannot be paid twice. Once settled, it is obliterated, effaced.

Jesus Christ paid our debt for us. He endured our pains, our diseases, and the judgment of our sins. We are redeemed to God. Our physical and spiritual slavery under Satan is ended. We are now the children of God.

The message of the gospel is good news.

The Sovereign Lord has filled me with his spirit. He has chosen me and sent me to bring good news to the poor, to heal the broken-hearted, to announce release to the captives and freedom to those in prison... Isa.61:1TEV

T.L. & Daisy were married on April 5, 1942, at the Full Gospel Church in Los Banos, California. Daisy departed this life on May 27, 1995.

ALL *THINGS ARE-POSSIBLE* IF THOU CANST ONLY BELIEVE MK 9:15

From their youth, T.L. and Daisy Osborn ministered together as a team in their world evangelism ministry—until Daisy's demise in 1995. Here are crutches, braces and other aids discarded by those miraculously healed during their first gospel tent campaign in Pennsylvania. God confirms His Word with *"signs, wonders and miracles."*

From the beginning of their half-century of ministry together, T.L. and Daisy Osborn pioneered *Mass Miracle Evangelism* as an effective way to demonstrate the gospel in *NON-Christian* nations. They may have shared Christ with more *UN-evangelized* people, witnessing more conversions and healing miracles than any couple in history.

T.L. and Daisy Osborn
Mass Miracle
Evangelism Crusades

HONDURAS – Tegucigalpa

JAPAN – Kyoto

EAST AFRICA – Mombasa, Kenya

PHILIPPINES – Davao, Mindanao

S. AMERICA – Bogota, Colombia

THE
HAROLD KHAN
MIRACLE

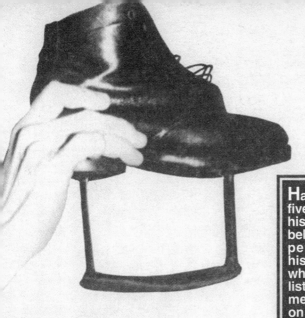

Harold's right leg was five inches shorter than his left one. The photo below shows both legs perfectly equal after his miraculous healing which took place as he listened to T.L.'s gospel message and believed on Christ. (His right elevated shoe and left leg brace are now obsolete.)

Both Harold's mother (standing with him above) and his father (devout Muslims) accepted Christ as their Savior and Lord.

T.L. and Daisy Osborn
Mass Miracle
Evangelism Crusades

WEST AFRICA – Accra, Ghana

MEXICO – Cuidad Juarez

AFRICA – Kampala, Uganda

CARIBBEAN – Ponce, Puerto Rico

TRINIDAD – San Fernando

The Osborns greet the people during their Hyderabad, India crusade where they proclaimed the gospel of Christ to multitudes of up to 300,000 people daily.

He has been unable to walk without crutches for seven years. Now he is completely healed.

This man has been blind for ten years. During the mass prayer after Dr. Osborn's message in the Hyderabad, India crusade, he received his sight and now wants the multitude to know that he has become a believer in Jesus Christ.

A spinal injury crippled this man, but he has accepted Christ and now is healed.

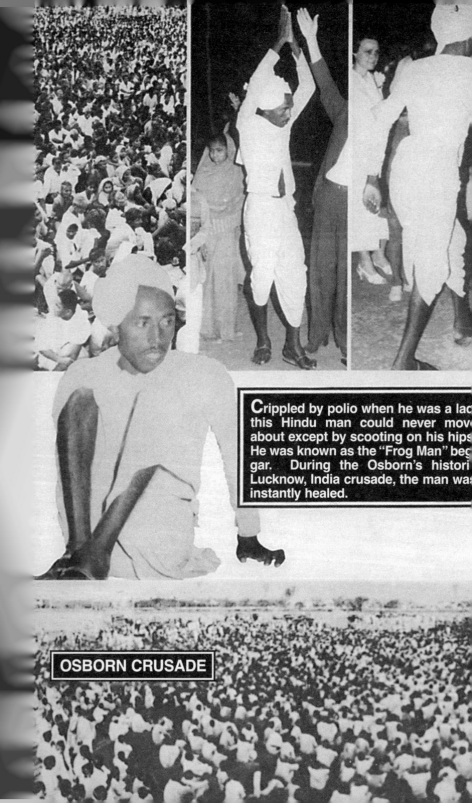

Crippled by polio when he was a lac[...] this Hindu man could never mov[...] about except by scooting on his hips[...] He was known as the "Frog Man" beg[...] gar. During the Osborn's histori[...] Lucknow, India crusade, the man wa[...] instantly healed.

OSBORN CRUSADE

Crippled by Infantile Paralysis, Shanti Sundram could only walk with a hip-to-ankle brace. One leg was 3 inches shorter than the other. She was miraculously healed during the Osborn Crusade at Madurai, India. (Top) Her mother thanks God for this miracle.

MADURAI, INDIA

THE JUAN SANTOS MIRACLE

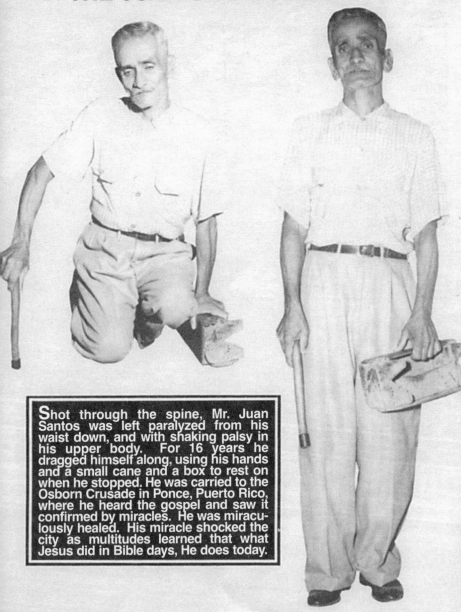

Shot through the spine, Mr. Juan Santos was left paralyzed from his waist down, and with shaking palsy in his upper body. For 16 years he dragged himself along, using his hands and a small cane and a box to rest on when he stopped. He was carried to the Osborn Crusade in Ponce, Puerto Rico, where he heard the gospel and saw it confirmed by miracles. He was miraculously healed. His miracle shocked the city as multitudes learned that what Jesus did in Bible days, He does today.

OSBORN CRUSADE

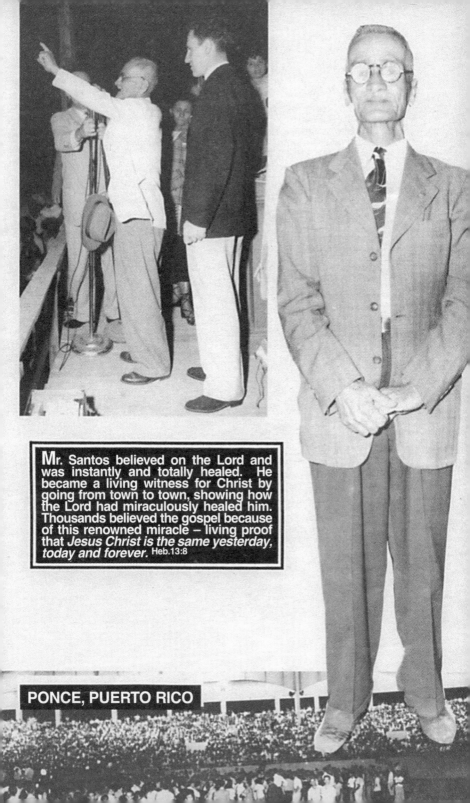

Mr. Santos believed on the Lord and was instantly and totally healed. He became a living witness for Christ by going from town to town, showing how the Lord had miraculously healed him. Thousands believed the gospel because of this renowned miracle – living proof that *Jesus Christ is the same yesterday, today and forever.* Heb.13:8

PONCE, PUERTO RICO

Dr. LaDonna's lifetime involvement in mass miracle evangelism has equipped her to minister with ease and great authority, as shown here during the Osborn Festivals of Faith & Miracles in Kupang, Waingapu and Palangkaraya, Indonesia.

LaDonna Osborn Gospel Seminar & Book Distribution

LaDonna Osborn Festival of Faith & Miracles – Kupang, Indonesia

LaDonna Osborn Festival of Faith & Miracles – Waingapu, Indonesia

LaDonna Osborn Festival of Faith & Miracles – Palangkaraya, Indonesia

Waingapu, indonesia

MUSLIM BEGGAR CRAWLED

"I am no longer a Muslim. I will follow Jesus Christ. He must be alive; otherwise how could He have done this miracle for me? The Christians' Bible must be true!"

OSBORN CRUSADE

FOR 30 YEARS

Karimu, a Muslim, crawled on the ground, from village to village in West Africa, begging for his living. He was a professional beggar.

Then he became a notable walking miracle, a living witness of God's Love-power for the thousands who had known of his condition.

He was miraculously healed during the Osborn Crusade in Ibadan, Nigeria. His testimony of healing is known throughout the nation – proof that Jesus Christ is ALIVE! He says, "I went many places with my wife and child, telling what God did for me. Some nights I never slept, so many wanted to talk to me and see me walk."

He asked Dr. Daisy for a new Christian name. She said, "Your new name will be *Cornelius.*"

NIGERIA

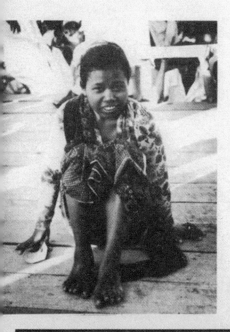

"I had a high fever and my feet swelled as big as they could without bursting. When the sickness left, I could not walk. My legs were useless. The only way I could get around was to scoot myself along on the ground with my hands.

"I attended the Osborn Crusade in Surabaya, Java. I arrived, scooting on the ground, at about two o'clock in the afternoon so that I could be close to the platform for the meeting. I wanted to be able to hear everything that was said.

"The third meeting that I attended, I believed what Mr. Osborn was telling us about this Jesus Christ. I followed the prayer the best that I could and I accepted Jesus as my Savior and resolved to follow Him. That day I was instantly healed. My legs became strong again, and I got up on my feet and walked as well as I ever could. I was restored and normal again. I thank the Lord Jesus Christ for healing me so that I can now walk again. I always want to serve him."

Kitnak Baluan

"**I** had a high fever for four days and was sick in bed for a month, suffering awful agony in my body, especially in my legs. I would just lay in bed and cry with pain in my legs.

"Then after that sickness and fever left me, I found that I could not stand up or walk. When I tried, my legs would not straighten out or hold me up. From that time, the only way I could move about was to use my hands and scoot along in the sitting position. I continued to suffer much pain.

"One day we heard some good news. We heard about the Osborn Crusade in Surabaya. I scooted on my hips all the way to that great meeting where a man by the name of Osborn was speaking to the people about God and Jesus Christ. I listened to him. He called it the *Gospel*. I believed this Jesus would help me. I was instantly healed.

"I have been a Muslim all of my life, but now I have accepted Jesus Christ as my Savior and I will serve Him always. I am perfectly healed and can walk as good as I ever could before I was sick. I am very thankful for this miracle by Jesus Christ."

Prauan Panjaman

HE WAS A LEPER

"Eighteen years ago, I went to the doctor for an examination. I had a white spot on my right shoulder. When he saw it, he sent me to a leprosy specialist who, after taking many tests, told me that I had leprosy.

"Immediately my family put me in a separate room. From then, I could only talk to them at a distance, and I had to eat, sleep and live alone.

"During the next year, my hands became swollen. I could not close my fingers. Bumps began to appear all over my body, and then my face began to swell.

"My eyes were nearly swollen shut, and my ears were double their normal size, and hung down at least an inch longer than usual. They were about as thick as my finger. They were terribly swollen and infected – and had no feeling.

"During the next few years my hands were so badly affected

*The Lepers are Cleansed.*Mt.11:

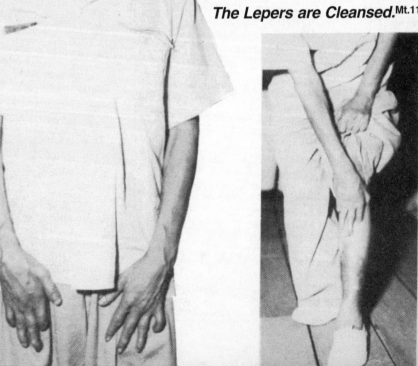

crippled and even incurable people were being miraculously cured by this Jesus.

"After attending for three nights and witnessing what was happening to others, I began to believe that I too could be helped. I decided to do as the man said, and I accepted Jesus Christ as my Savior and I purposed to follow Him according to the Bible.

"While I was following in the prayer being led by Mr. Osborn, I suddenly felt something in my hands. I found that I could open and close them – this I had not done for years.

"Then I realized that I was being healed. In one week I was perfectly whole. My skin is clean. The ulcer on my leg and the other sores are dried up and gone. Life has returned to all of my body and I am clean within and without.

"None of us were Christians, and never planned to be, but we had never seen Christ's power to cleanse lepers before.

"Oh, it is wonderful! My wife and I are reunited now, and can eat at the same table and live together as a husband and wife should.

"All of my family have accepted Christ, and we are all following Him, and we shall serve Him all the days of our lives."

Priok Rimbanguan

that I lost the first joints of my forefinger on my right hand. Then five years ago, a big sore started on my left shin near the ankle. It increased until it must have been more than 12 inches long and nearly encircled my leg which was terribly swollen, and it drained continually.

"By that time, I had bumps and sores all over my body, and the odor was strong and offensive.

"A strange thing happened. A man and woman came to Djakarta, my city, held great meetings on a big field in the center of the city. They talked about Jesus Christ and said He was the Savior of the world, and that He would forgive our sins and heal our bodies.

"I was persuaded to attend the Osborn Crusade where the public was saying that sick and

T.L. & DAISY OSBORN CRUSADES. For over a half-century, they were pace-setters in mass-evangelism, sharing Christ with more people in *non-Christian* nations than any couple in history. Since Daisy's demise in 1995, T.L. has continued his ministry across Russia, Poland, Belarus, Ukraine, Lithuania, Eurasia, Latin America, French speaking Africa and India, anticipating the opening of China, N. Korea and Mongolia.

Dr. LaDonna Osborn has been involved with her parents in miracle evangelism from her youth. The same anointing that has rested upon T.L. and Daisy, is evident in LaDonna's own global ministry. As the gospel is proclaimed by either T.L. or LaDonna, crutches, canes, braces and wheelchairs are hoisted to signal miracles received through the power of God's word. As in Jesus' day, *The power of the Lord was present to heal.* Lu. 5:17

LaDonna and T.L. strategize global crusades and literature-distribution. Their preaching is always confirmed by miracles. TONS of their books seed church leaders and believers for spiritual harvests, impacting nations with Christ's gospel.

"What Christ's power and love have done for others, it will do in your life. This book contains the seven miracle keys of *Biblical Healing* for YOU."
LaDonna and T.L. Osborn

Signs, wonders and miracles confirm the ministry of Dr. LaDonna as she promulgates the healing gospel in her global crusades.

Ugandan preacher, blind for 20 years, receives his sight and weeps reverently, then bursts into tearful laughter, as he looks and sees with his restored eyes.

This Muslim man was totally blind. As Dr. Daisy ministers to the multitude at the Municipal Stadium grounds at Mombasa, Kenya, he believes on Christ, accepts Him into his life and immediately his eyes receive sight. He tells everyone of the wonderful miracle he has received and publicly pledges to follow this Jesus who has restored his sight.

WOMEN'S NATIONAL CONFERENCE – E. AFRICA

Daisy Osborn seeds the women of the world in her national women's mass rallies abroad.

INDONESIAN WOMEN'S DAY – SURABAYA

WOMEN'S NATIONAL MIRACLE DAY – KAMPALA

AUSTRALIAN CONFERENCE

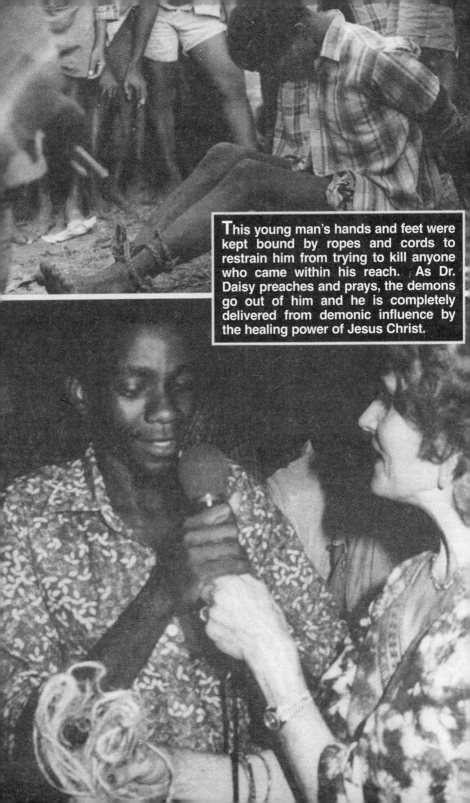

This young man's hands and feet were kept bound by ropes and cords to restrain him from trying to kill anyone who came within his reach. As Dr. Daisy preaches and prays, the demons go out of him and he is completely delivered from demonic influence by the healing power of Jesus Christ.

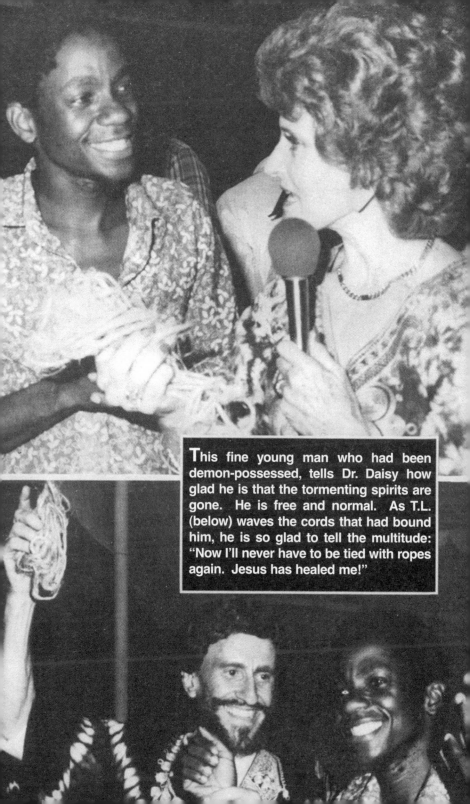

This fine young man who had been demon-possessed, tells Dr. Daisy how glad he is that the tormenting spirits are gone. He is free and normal. As T.L. (below) waves the cords that had bound him, he is so glad to tell the multitude: "Now I'll never have to be tied with ropes again. Jesus has healed me!"

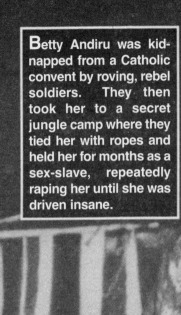

Betty Andiru was kidnapped from a Catholic convent by roving, rebel soldiers. They then took her to a secret jungle camp where they tied her with ropes and held her for months as a sex-slave, repeatedly raping her until she was driven insane.

For 13 years Betty was like an animal. She would bark like a dog and fight anyone who got near her. Friends managed to bring her to the Osborn Crusade. After Dr. Daisy preached and prayed for the mass of people, Betty was instantly restored, and she has since become an evangelist.

At the Lugogo Stadium, Betty Andiru relates to Dr. Daisy, and to the public, the wonder of her miraculous healing. In a moving witness of God's love-power, she tells how Jesus brought forgiveness into her heart for the rebels who had brutalized her until she went mad. She appeals to everyone to forgive whoever has wronged them during Uganda's civil war.

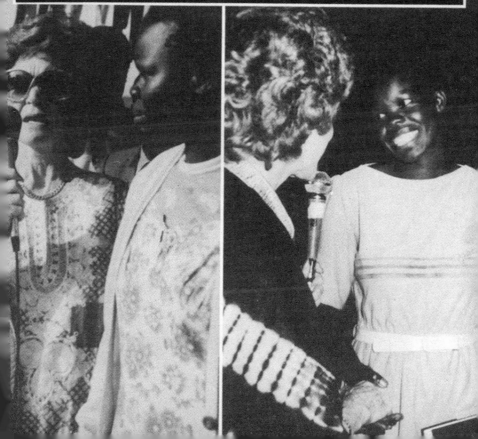

DYNAMIC GOSPEL SEED

KYRGYZSTAN

POLAND

GEORGIA

LATVIA

BELARUS

UKRAINE

RUSSIA

SIBERIA

UZBEKISTAN

ARM

From the North, East, South and West of Eurasia, women and men gather in Moscow from 212 cities, towns and villages, to hear Dr. LaDonna Osborn share evangelism keys for reaching their nations with the gospel.

Lenin and Stalin's Communism did not work. The gospel of the resurrected Jesus brings hope and life, healing and dignity wherever it is proclaimed and demonstrated.

Dr. LaDonna preaches to thousands of women and men from all corners of Russia during her Moscow conference.

OWN ACROSS EURASIA

KOLSKIY PENINSULA

BASHKORTOSTAN

TATARSTAN

KHAKASSIA

ABKHAZIA

KAZAKHSTAN UDMURTIA KARELIA URAL REGION

In Russia alone, there are 36,000 totally unreached villages. In Kazakhstan, there are 14 million people who have never heard of Jesus. The harvest is RIPE! The time is NOW!

Dr. LaDonna's focus is reaching the unreached, and establishing them as vibrant ambassadors of Christ, expressing His love-power to others.

Pastor of a large, new church & Bible School in Siberia.

This woman believer learns truths that build her faith in God.

She writes feverishly to avoid missing any nugget of truth.

T.L. Osborn ministers the miracle Gospel in Moscow, Russia.

Tons of Osborn books are given to believers in the Antioquia Province of S. America.

T.L. Osborn

T.L. Osborn ministers under Eckman's 10,000 seat tent, Sweden.

Only miracles can convince the ex-Soviet nations about Christ.

After Daisy's death, the Osborn daughter, Dr. LaDonna ministered with her father in their trans-evangelical seminar and public miracle crusade in Medellin, Colombia.

LaDonna Osborn

Swedes; famous for Missions, respond to T.L.'s dynamic preaching.

Miracles of healing confirm the preaching of the gospel in the Osborn Crusades across Latin America, such as these photos depict in their Monterrey, Mexico Crusade.

Her leg was 4 inches shorter than the other, and paralyzed — the result of a birth defect. She was instantly healed in the Osborn Crusade at Bogota, Colombia.

Dr. Osborn seldom preached a message during the Monterrey, Mexico Crusade without being interrupted by someone in the audience who received a MIRACLE and hoisted crutches or canes or braces as they came pressing through the throng toward the platform to give public testimony of what God had done for them.

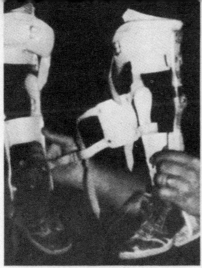

This eight-year old girl could not walk without leg braces and special shoes. During Dr. Osborn's message, her mother removed the shoes and braces and the child could walk. She came to the platform and walked its full length without faltering. Below, Dr. Daisy holds the girl up for the audience to see while the mother explains the miracle.

T.L. and Daisy Osborn listen as Peter Amakanji relates the pathetic story of 23 years as a beggar. He said, "I had a fever when I was a child, and have never had legs that I could walk on. I scooted myself backward, on my hips, with my hands, dragging my legs like wet ropes." He was brought to the Osborn Crusade in Nakuru, Kenya. As he sat on the ground amidst 75,000 standing people, he heard the gospel, was miraculously healed and immediately began to witness to people publicly and one-to-one. He assisted in some of Osborns' later crusades, bringing numerous cripples to the meetings where they were saved and healed.

The Osborns rejoice with Kariuki (left), a former maniac who was healed in their Kikuyuland Crusade, and with Peter Amakanji (center) the former paralytic who had dragged on the ground for 23 years. These are two notable wonders of God in East Africa.

INSET: "Look what God did for me!" Peter tells a crippled woman to come to the Osborn Crusade where she too can be healed.

The woman came and was miraculously healed. Peter was there to rejoice with her and to confirm that he had witnessed to her.

This lad is hoisted above the shoulders of those who saw him take his first miracle steps following T.L.'s message and mass prayer for healing. He is brought through the crowd, to the platform in Nakuru, where all can see the wonder of his miracle.

INSET: As the multitude looked with amazement, the young man, with the steel brace and shoes lifted high, marched across the platform to show the miracle God had done for him.

Just as in Bible days, Dr. LaDonna goes and preaches everywhere, the Lord working with her and confirming the word through the accompanying signs. (Mk 16:20 paraphrased)

The cripples are walking. The blind are seeing. The deaf are hearing. Cancers are disappearing. Hundreds of physical healing miracles are confirming the message of God's love and saving plan for people.

God never left himself without a witness; there are always his reminders...Ac.14:17 LB

T.L. AND DAISY OSBORN
Ambassadors of God's healing Love during more than a half-century of global miracle evangelism ministry together before Daisy's demise in 1995.

Damiano was a crippled beggar. During the Osborn Crusade in Uganda, T.L. prays for him – and shows him love. Damiano shows the people how he can now walk, as T.L. holds his sticks. Below, dressed in new clothes provided by local pastors, Damiano is proud to stand with T.L. and Daisy – the ones who brought him the good news of God's healing Love.

OSBORN MINISTRIES –

- Angola
- Argentina
- Armenia
- Australia
- Austria
- Azerbaijan
- Bangladesh
- Belarus
- Belgium
- Benin
- Bermuda
- Bolivia
- Botswana
- Brazil
- Bulgaria
- Burkina Faso
- Burundi

- Cambodia
- Cameroon
- Canada
- Central Afr. Rep.
- Chad
- Chile
- China
- Colombia
- Congo (Dem. Rep.)
- Congo (Rep.)
- Costa Rica
- Cuba
- Denmark
- Dominican Rep.
- Ecuador
- Egypt
- El Salvador
- England
- Estonia
- Ethiopia
- Finland
- France
- Gabon

- Georgia
- Germany
- Ghana
- Guatemala
- Haiti
- Honduras

LEGEND

Nations in which the Osborns
have proclaimed the Gospel
in face-to-face ministry.

OVER 60 YEARS – OVER 100 NATIONS

- Hong Kong
- India
- Indonesia
- Ireland
- Italy
- Ivory Coast
- Jamaica
- Japan
- Kazakhstan
- Kenya
- Kyrgyzstan
- Laos
- Liberia
- Lithuania
- Luxemborg
- Madagascar
- Malawi
- Malaysia
- Mexico
- Mongolia
- Myanmar
- Netherlands

- New Zealand
- Nicaragua
- Nigeria
- Norway
- Pakistan
- Panama
- Papua N.Guinea
- Paraguay
- Peru
- Philippines
- Poland
- Portugal
- Puerto Rico
- Russia

- Rwanda
- Senegal
- South Africa
- South Korea
- Spain
- Sri Lanka
- Sweden
- Switzerland
- Taiwan
- Tajikistan
- Tanzania
- Thailand
- Togo
- Trinidad
- Uganda
- Ukraine
- United States
- Uruguay
- Uzbekistan
- Venezuela
- Vietnam
- Virgin Islands
- Zambia

T.L. & LaDonna Osborn Miracle Crusade—Medellin, Colombia

LaDonna Osborn

T.L. & LaDonna Osborn Miracle-Life Conference—Amlaty, Kyrghyzstan, an ex-Soviet Republic. The 10 Osborn books in Russian are given to every adult.

T.L. & Daisy Osborn Mass Miracle Crusade – Bogota, S. America

Thousands attend the T.L. & LaDonna Osborn *Miracle Life* Conference in this ancient Muslim nation of Kyrghyzstan–bordering West China.

T.L. Osborn

Christ's Ministry of Healing Continues Today...

Dr.T.L. Osborn   Dr.LaDonna Osborn

...through PUBLIC MIRACLE CRUSADES in over 100 countries

...through GOSPEL MATERIALS in over 130 languages worldwide

...through teaching the promises of God in PUBLIC SEMINARS

...through EQUIPPING BELIEVERS WORLDWIDE for evangelism

...through PRAYER & INTERCESSION for Partners & the World

Part

IV

JESUS

❧

THE
HEALING
LIFE

THE FOURTH STEP to receive BIBLICAL HEALING is to understand that physical healing is a part of salvation.

Chapter 13

The Savior Is The Healer

WE CANNOT SEPARATE
Jesus, *The Healer* from Jesus, *The Savior*.

So, we cannot separate
BIBLICAL HEALING from *biblical salvation*.

The best way to receive healing from Christ for your physical body is to welcome Jesus, *The Healer*, into your life.

If you called a medical expert to aid your suffering loved one, you would welcome the physician into their house.

In a quest for Christ's healing, you would begin by welcoming *The Healer* into your own life.

We have had the joy of seeing thousands of people miraculously healed of all manner of diseases and physical disabilities. Always, before we pray for physical healing, we help those who are sick (if unconverted) to receive Jesus Christ into their lives—to welcome Him as their savior and Lord. After receiving *The Healer*, they can then receive His healing for their physical needs.

Receive Christ—
Receive *The Healer*

A man seeking healing for an incurable disease attended our crusade for several days. He had never received Christ as his savior. Although he had no interest in Christ, the gravity of his illness caused him to repeat the healing prayer each night. The dear man received no answer because he wanted healing without *The Healer*.

Finally the word of God convinced him of his sins and of his need to receive Jesus as his savior. Later he testified: "I decided to receive Christ as Lord of my life and as I prayed for Him to come into my life, I was wonderfully saved. Then I heard Mr. Osborn tell the multitude that the Lord who had saved us from our sins would now heal us of our diseases. I suddenly realized that *He had already healed me.*"

That man had prayed many nights to be healed but had rejected *The Healer*. When he decided to receive Jesus as his Lord and savior, Christ healed him before he had a chance to ask. The Bible says, *He forgiveth all thine iniquities, He healeth all thy diseases.*[Psa.103:3]

Another unconverted man came to our crusade

in great physical need. He had two ruptures, and one deaf ear. He responded to Christ in the first meeting that he attended and was gloriously saved.

While he was thanking God for salvation from his sins, Christ *The Healer*, who had been welcomed into his life, healed his body completely — before he ever asked for physical healing.

He Was Saved—
His Blindness Left

A blind gentleman was led to one of our crusades. He stood amidst the multitude and listened to the gospel. He believed the message of Christ, repented of his sins and received the Lord Jesus into his heart. He was instantly healed of his blindness when *The Healer* entered his life.

He rushed forward to give public witness of the miracle he had received. He wept as he told his story and said: "Jesus has come into my life. He is right here in my heart." Pounding his chest, he urged, "Lay your hand here, you can feel Him. He is here. I can see everything. He has opened my blind eyes. I am saved. I am healed."

God's order for blessing our lives is that He *forgives all our iniquities,* [and then He] *heals all our diseases.*[Psa.103:3] Forgiveness for our sins comes first, then healing for our diseases follows.

A paralytic was lowered through an opening in the roof and was laid before Christ. He said to the man, *Your sins are forgiven you.* Then He added, *Arise, take up your bed, and go your way into your house.*[Mk.2:5-11] It was forgiveness first, and then physical healing followed.

God's condition for His healing covenant is, *You shall serve the Lord your God...*then He adds *and I will take sickness away from the midst of you.* [Ex.23:25]

Healing comes from *The Healer.* He heals from within. When we receive Him, we receive His healing in our physical bodies because health is part of His abundant *Life.*[Jn.10:10]

How could one receive healing while rejecting *The Healer?*

A man asked, "Will you pray for me to be healed?"

"Certainly," I replied, and then I asked, "Have you received Jesus Christ as Lord and savior of your life?"

"No!" was his reply.

"Then," I asked, "why do you ask God to heal you when you do not love Him enough to serve Him? Why should you ask Him for more strength to serve the devil? If you serve God, He will heal your body, but if you refuse to serve Him by refusing to receive Christ into your life, you should not expect Him to heal you."

The man thought this over intelligently, made

his decision, accepted Christ as Lord and savior, was joyfully converted, and was instantly healed.

If you might be one who desires physical healing but have never received Jesus Christ into your life,[Jn.3:7,17; Lu.9:56; Rom.10:13; 1Tim.1:15] now is the time to be saved.

> *Now is the accepted time, behold, now is the day of salvation.*[2Cor.6:2]

Miracle of The New Birth

The Bible says: *All have sinned, and come short of the glory of God,*[Rom.3:23] [and] *Except you repent, you shall all likewise perish.*[Lu.13:5]

It says, *Your iniquities have separated between you and your God, and your sins have hid his face from you, that he will not hear.*[Isa.59:2]

But it also says that Christ's blood was *shed for many for the remission of sins,*[Mat.26:28] [and] *you shall call his name JESUS: for he shall save his people from their sins.*[Mat.1:21] *If we confess our sins [to him], he is faithful and just to forgive us our sins, and to cleanse us from all unrighteousness.*[1Jn.1:9]

According to these scriptures, if one has not accepted Christ's forgiveness for his or her sins, that person is separated from God who will not hear their prayers. But through His shed blood, all can have remission and cleansing for sins [Mat.26:28; Eph.1:7;]

1Jn.1:7; Rev.1:5 if they humble themselves, Jas.4:10 confess their sins to Him,1Jn.1:9 and receive Him as their savior and Lord.Jn.1:12

Jesus said, *You must be born again,* Jn.3:7 and Paul said, *If any one be in Christ, he or she is a new creature; old things are passed away; behold, all things are become new.*2Cor.5:17

This is the miracle of the new birth.

**Christ enters our lives,
and we are made new
because He comes to live in us.**

**He is a person, not a philosophy—
a reality, not a religion.**

When I was married, I accepted my wife into my life. I did not get the "marriage religion;" I became *one* with another person, my wife. And when I was saved or reborn by receiving Christ into my life, I did not get the "Christian religion." I became *one* with another person, the Lord Jesus. My conversion was as definite as my marriage was. In both cases I received another person into my life.

When we understand what salvation means, then to say, "I do not know for sure if I am saved," is as unreasonable as to say, "I do not know for sure if I am married."

Some who do not understand salvation, when asked if they are saved, may reply: "I think so; I try to be, but I am not sure about it." That is like saying, "I think I am married; I try to be, but I am not sure about it."

John said, *We **know** that we have passed from death unto life.*[1Jn.3:14] There are many things which we may never know, but we can *know* that we have received Christ's life. We can *know* that we have been saved — that we are born again. (Read my books, GOD'S LOVE PLAN and NEW MIRACLE LIFE NOW.)

You Shall Be Saved

Some may ask: "How can I know that I am saved? How can I be sure that my sins are forgiven?"

A Philippian jailer asked: *What must I do to be saved?* Paul and Silas *said, Believe on the Lord Jesus Christ, and you shall be saved.*[Ac.16:30-31]

Jesus said, *Those that believe* [the gospel] *and are baptized, shall be saved.*[Mk.16:16]

Paul said, *If you shall confess with your mouth Jesus as Lord, and shall believe in your heart that God has raised him from the dead, you shall be saved.*[Rom.10:9]

Peter said, *Whoever shall call on the name of the Lord shall be saved.*[Ac.2:21]

Every one of these scriptures contains the promise,

"*shall be saved.*" When people do what these scriptures say, they can know that they have received Christ, that they *have passed from death to life,* Jn.5:24 [that they are] *born again.* Jn.3:7; 1Pet.1:23; 1Jn.5:4

Chapter 14

God's Love-Plan

HERE IS AN outline for understanding God's love-plan of salvation.

I. The Principle of Self-Value

A. We are created in God's image to share His life, love and purpose and we are therefore infinitely valuable to Him.

1. *For we are God's workmanship.*Eph.2:10

2. *God created humankind in his own image, in the image of God created he him, male and female created he them.*Gen.1:27

3. *The Lord made humankind a little lower than God,* [King James Version—*"angels,"* Original Hebrew, French and certain other language-versions—*"God."*] *and crowned him with glory and honor, and made him to have dominion over the works of his hands; and has put all things under his feet.*Psa.8:5-6

II. The Basic Problem in Human Life

A. Adam and Eve chose to not trust God's word.

1. *And the Lord commanded, Of every tree of the garden you may freely eat: but of the tree of the knowledge of good and evil, you will not eat of it: for in the day that you eat of it **you will surely die**.*^{Gen.2:16-17}

2. Satan contradicted God and said, *You will **not** surely die.*^{Gen.3:4}

   a. He influenced them to distrust God's word.

3. *Eve took of the fruit and ate it, and gave some to her husband with her; and he ate it.*^{Gen.3:6}

> ## That was the original sin:
> ## — Distrusting GOD'S Word —

III. **The Negative Power of Unbelief**

A. To question God's integrity produces deterioration and death in the human race.

1. *God said, in the day that you disavow my instructions and eat the fruit that I forbade, you will surely die.*^{Gen.2:17LT}

2. *The wages of sin* [disavowing the integrity of God's word] *is death.*^{Rom.6:23}

3. *Whereas, by one person sin entered into the world, and death by sin; so death passed upon all persons, for that all have sinned.* Rom.5:12

IV. The Love-Plan of God for Us

A. God loved and valued us too much to let us die; He gave Jesus to be judged and condemned in our place, to exonerate us from all guilt.

1. *God was not willing that any should perish but that all should come to repentance.*2Pet.3:9

2. *God so loved the world that he gave his only begotten Son, that whoever believes in him will not perish, but have everlasting life.* Jn.3:16

3. *God showed his great love for us by sending Christ to die for us.*Rom.5:8LB

4. *Now God says He will accept and acquit us—declare us not guilty—if we trust Jesus Christ to take away our sins. For God sent Christ Jesus to take the punishment for our sins and to end all of God's anger against us. Our acquittal is not based on our good deeds; it is based on what Christ has done and our faith in him.* Rom.3:21,25,27LB

a. Since no debt can be paid twice, or no crime punished twice, we can be restored to God as though we have never committed sin.

b. Since Jesus Christ suffered the penalty that we deserved, and since He did it on our behalf, we are no longer guilty before God and can never be judged for the sins that we have committed, because the judgment we deserved was put on Jesus, our substitute and that judgment can never be imposed on us again.

B. That was God's love-plan to save us and to restore us to the life that He designed us for.

V. The Secret of Identity with Christ

A. We are restored to God's life when we commit our lives to Jesus Christ and receive Him.

B. When we identify with what He did for us and when we believe that He assumed the judgment of our sins, in our place, this is what occurs:

1. The righteousness of Christ is transferred to our account and we are free of all guilt and judgment.

2. Jesus Christ comes and lives the life of God in and through us.

3. We become new creations.

4. We are restored to God according to His original plan.

5. A supernatural power is given to us that makes us children of God. It is a miracle.

   a. *God made Jesus Christ who knew no sin to be made sin on our behalf, so that in him we might share the righteousness [or life] of God.*2Cor.5:21

   b. *As many as receive Jesus Christ, God gives them power to become the children of God.*Jn.1:12

   c. *If anyone is in Christ, he or she is a new creature. All things become new.* 2Cor.5:17

   d. *Jesus said, I am come that you might have life more abundantly.* Jn.10:10

C. In receiving Christ, we are restored to friendship, fellowship and *Life* with God as we were designed for in the beginning.

> ***Truly our fellowship is with the Father, and with his Son, Jesus Christ.*** 1Jn.1:3

Chapter 15

Receive The Healer

BECAUSE THIS fourth step to receive BIBLICAL HEALING is so essential to salvation, we must clearly understand what it means to receive Jesus Christ by faith.

According to the Bible, this thing that we call *faith* is the most important of all. It means to *only believe* Mk.5:36 what Jesus said.

To be saved is to receive the life of Christ. One must know the promises of God for salvation, and put complete trust in what Jesus accomplished for every human person through His sacrificial death on the cross, His burial, his resurrection and His ascension back to the Father.

To receive Christ, it is not enough to recognize one's sins, to abhor them and to repent of them; it is not enough to ask forgiveness and make promises and resolutions to live a Christian life, or even to say with one's lips that one has accepted Christ.

It is by an act of *faith* that we receive Jesus and make Him the LORD of our life.

*The gospel is the power of God to salvation, to every one that believes.*Rom.1:16

By grace [unmerited favor] *are we saved through faith; and that not of ourselves: it is the gift of God: not of works, lest any one should boast.*Eph.2:8-9

For they that come to God must believe that he is, and that he is a rewarder of them that diligently seek him. Heb.11:6

*Without faith it is impossible to please him.*Heb.11:6

The Bible promises *Whoever shall call upon the name of the Lord shall be saved,*Rom.10:13 and this salvation can only be accepted *by faith.*

What Faith Means

Faith is believing that what God said is true.

Faith means that we expect God to do what He promised to do. That is why *faith comes by hearing...the word of God.*Rom.10:17 We must know what God has promised to do before we can expect Him to do it.

> **Once we know God's promises and expect Him to fulfill them,** *that is faith.*

Faith is accepting God's promises and being so convinced that they are true that we act upon them — even in the face of circumstances or evidence that seems contrary.

175

What are we to believe? *The gospel* — the Good News of what Jesus accomplished for us through His death, burial, resurrection and ascension.

Jesus said, *Have faith in God.*[Mk.11:22] We are to accept these statements about Christ and His sacrifice for us [1Cor.15:1-4] as being true, whether they seem reasonable or not. *That is faith.*

The Bible says that *He was wounded for our transgressions, he was bruised for our iniquities.*[Isa.53:5] *Who his own self bore our sins in his own body on the tree, that we being dead to sins, should live to righteousness.*
[1Pet.2:24]

For God made him [Jesus] *to be sin for us, who knew no sin; that we might be made the righteousness of God in him.*[2Cor.5:21]

These statements seem incredible. Human logistics cannot rationalize as fact that the sins we have committed, and the sicknesses we may feel, were placed on Jesus Christ two thousand years ago, and that he put them away. *Faith* means that we believe these facts of the gospel without trying to rationalize them. And when we *believe them*, God confirms His word and miracles result.

The *mystery* of the gospel is:

1. Christ died *for us* and endured the penalty of our sins — they were charged to His account.

2. Now our debt is paid in full and no longer exists — it is expunged.

Why did our Lord do this?

Because we had sinned against God and had broken His law which declares:

*The soul that sins shall die,*Eze.18:20 and *The wages of sin is death.*Rom.6:23

God loved us too much to let us die.

That is why He saved us — He redeemed us.

Beginning of the Problem

Man and woman were created perfect, sinless, healthy, pure, happy — and they lived in a garden of plenty. They walked and talked with God and had no sense of inferiority, condemnation, guilt or fear.

Then Satan's temptation came. Adam and Eve disobeyed God and ate the forbidden fruit.Gen.3:1-6 That was sin which resulted in death.

*Wherefore, as by one, sin entered into the world, and death by sin; so death passed upon all, for that all have sinned.*Rom.5:12

Adam and Eve were separated from God's presence to live forever as slaves of Satan. The terrible consequences of their sin — evil, hatred, envy, greed, murder, disease, heartache, failure, pain, poverty, defeat and all the works of the devil — began devastating the human race.

God's law, which demanded that all who sin must die, could not be changed; yet, *He was not willing that any should perish, but that all should come* to repentance.[2Pet.3:9] *He has no pleasure in the death of them that die.*[Eze.18:32]

So...*He so loved the world, that he gave his only begotten Son, that whoever believes in him should not perish, but have everlasting life.*[Jn.3:16]

Jesus came to our level and lived as a human person, but without sin. He could therefore become our substitute and could assume the penalty and the judgment of our sins in our place.

We could not pay for our own sins and live, because our penalty is death. All had sinned, so all had to die. That is why Jesus came. He had not sinned. He was conceived by a miracle of the Holy Spirit in which a divine seed was planted in the womb of Mary.[Lu.1:28-32,35]

The Man Without Sin

Since the blood comes from the father's seed, the blood of Christ was divine. His life was divine. *The life of the flesh is in the blood.*[Lev.17:11] Jesus was God in the flesh. The prophet said: *Call his name Emmanuel, which being interpreted is, God with us.*[Mat.1:23]

That is why John pointed to Him and said: *Behold the Lamb of God, which takes away the sin of the world.*[Jn.1:29]

When He was condemned and crucified on our behalf, He was our perfect and sinless substitute, taking our place in death, assuming our judgment. God's Son, with divine blood, died for us.

God said, *I have given the blood to you upon the altar to make atonement for the soul.*[Lev.17:11]

Jesus said, *This is my blood of the new testament, which is shed for many for the remission of sins.*[Mat.26:28]

Isaiah said, *The Lord laid on him* [Jesus] *the iniquity of us all,*[Isa.53:6] and *for the transgression of my people was he stricken.*[Isa.53:8] *His soul was made an offering for sin* [Isa.53:10] and *He bore their iniquity.*[Isa.53:11] *He bore the sin of many, and made intercession for the transgressors.*[Isa.53:12] That was for you and for me.

Faith in the Good News

Although this may seem incredible and unacceptable, this is the Good News by which we are saved.[1Cor.15:1]

People do not understand the north or south poles and have never *seen* them, but they accept their reality. Anyone who has traveled by plane or crossed the oceans by ship, has been guided by their influence.

Most people do not understand their radio, telephone, or other electronics, but they rely on them and put them to daily use.

In that same way, we believe the Good News of Jesus Christ; we believe that He took our place, suffered our pain and endured the judgment and penalty of our sins. And the result is, we are saved because we are believers.

When Christ died on the cross, He said, *it is finished*.[Jn.19-30]

- Our salvation was completed.
- Our debt can never be paid twice.
- Our penalty can never be imposed again.

Jesus assumed our guilt, in our stead, and our salvation is a present reality when we believe the gospel.

Trusting Christ

Do we have faith in what Jesus did for us? We must determine whether or not we *believe* the gospel message.

How can we prove our faith in Him? The answer is in a simple word: TRUST. We *trust* Him.

An old hymn has wonderful words:

'Tis so sweet to *trust* in Jesus,
Just to take Him at His word;
Just to know that we can *trust* Him,
Just to know, Thus saith the Lord.

I SAY TO the thousands who accept Christ in our mass crusades:

TRUST in the finished work of Christ for your spirit.

TRUST what He did all in your name.

TRUST that He suffered enough and paid the penalty for all of the sins that you ever committed.

TRUST that He was innocent so that He could take your place as your substitute.

TRUST that His blood was enough to wash away every sin; that nothing else needs to be done — that no additional price needs to be paid — that no other penalty needs to be endured — that no good works or offerings or merits or sacrifices or penance need to be added to what Christ did to redeem you.

TRUST that He did *enough*.

**Rest your faith forever
on the foundation of what the Bible says
that Jesus accomplished *for you*.**

Once we have heard and believed the Good News —

Once we have recognized our sins and have repented of them —

Once we have confessed and turned our back on them —

Once we have come to God and have asked His pardon, expressing our faith in what Jesus did for us —

Once we have accepted Him into our heart by faith —

Once we have decided to live for Him —

Once we have purposed to strive to please Him in all that we think and say and do:

Then never again do we need to do anything or make any sacrifice or effort or pay any price or take any other step, whatsoever, to be saved.

- We TRUST in Jesus Christ.

- We TRUST that He did enough at the cross.

- We TRUST His sacrifice.

- We TRUST that He paid our debt.

- We TRUST that He suffered enough.

- We TRUST His payment for our sins.
  Our offerings and good works will never improve our state of salvation.

- We TRUST in the blood of God's Son.

- We TRUST in His love to reach us, and in His power to redeem us.

- We TRUST in what He did at the cross.
  Nothing we can think or say or do now, or in the future, can add to what He did to ransom and to save us.

Jesus paid enough. He suffered enough. Our penance or offerings cannot add to what He accomplished on our behalf. He did it for us, in our name, so that we will never have to do anything more but *only believe.*Mk.5:36; Jn.9:38; 11:27;14:1,10; 19:35; 20:31; Ac.8:37; 13:39; 16:31; Rom.10:9-10

Keep Trusting

When we face our last day on earth, and draw

our last breath, in that moment we shall keep on TRUSTING. We shall not try to think or say or do anything to improve our salvation at that hour. What Jesus did over 2,000 years ago was enough. Our trust will rest in what He did on our behalf. We know we are saved. This is what the Bible means by *faith*. This is the Christian's greatest hour of triumph.

When we think of standing before God, let us not contemplate the value of anything that we ever thought or said or did as having any merit for our salvation.[Isa.64:6; Jer.2:22; Psa.49:6-7]

We shall depend only on what Jesus did for us, in our name, on the cross. We shall remember that He died in our place and that in His death, he *purged us from our sins.*[Heb.1:3]

Christ's own blood...obtained eternal redemption for us.[Heb.9:11-12,14; 10:19-22] His word says that the blood and righteousness of Jesus have been ascribed to our account and that God will only look at us and judge us *in Christ.* In other words, all of our sins have been charged to Christ's account, and all of Christ's righteousness has been credited to our account.

The Great Exchange

The paraphrased Living Bible translates this great Bible verse: *For God took the sinless Christ and poured into him our sins. Then in exchange, he poured God's goodness into us.*[2Cor.5:21]

When our faith is in Christ, we are calm, we are secure, we have no fear, we are at peace, because we trust in Jesus. We believe that He did *enough* for us. That is faith.

Believe on the Lord Jesus Christ, and you shall be saved.[Ac.16:31]

They that work not, but believe on him that justifies the ungodly, their faith is counted for righteousness. Rom.4:5

Therefore being justified by faith, we have peace with God through our Lord Jesus Christ.[Rom.5:1]

For by grace are you saved through faith; and that not of yourselves: it is the gift of God.[Eph.2:8]

You can seal your experience with God forever by confessing your faith in Him and in His word. If you have never received Christ as your savior, pray this prayer of confession to God now:

Prayer

DEAR LORD: Here and now, I believe on Jesus Christ, the Son of God. I believe that in Your great mercy and love, You died for me, as my substitute.

I believe that You suffered the penalty of my sins and paid the full price to redeem me to God.

You did no wrong. I was the sinner. The penalty of death was upon me. I should have been crucified. Even though I was separated

from You by my sins and iniquities,[Isa.59:2] You saw me in my fallen state and You loved me.

Lord Jesus, I thank You for paying my debt in full. Your blood was shed for the remission of my sins.

All of my sins were charged to Your account and You paid for me. Now all of Your righteousness is credited to my account so that I am now redeemed and saved.

I receive You into my life by faith. Now I am a new creature with the divine life of Jesus Christ.

I shall never make another effort, or claim any merit, or pay any price, or offer any good works, nor shall I ever—as long as I live— think or say or do anything more to have my sins forgiven, or to be saved.

From this day, I trust in what You did for me at the cross. It is enough.

Your blood cleanses me. I have Your life and I am saved now. From this moment I shall follow You and I shall strive to share the Good News with others so that they too can receive Your life.

Thank You, Lord, for my full salvation. AMEN!

Chapter 16

Your New Life Begins

NOW THAT YOU have prayed the prayer in the previous chapter, your new life begins. Jesus Christ has come into your life. You have received the greatest miracle that any person can experience—the life of Jesus Christ.

Your sins have been punished at the cross. Jesus suffered in your place. He paid the full price for your sins and endured the judgment they deserved. Those sins can never condemn you again. They are gone—like an old debt that, once paid, no longer exists.

You are not saved because of what you may have done, or ever can do. *By grace* [unmerited favor] *are you saved through faith; and that not of yourself: it is a gift of God: not of works, lest any one should boast.*Eph.2:8-9

The Way to Live in Faith

If you ever question your salvation, re-read the previous chapter, *Receive The Healer*. Ponder each verse of scripture in that chapter and guard them in your heart.

The Bible says: *They overcame* [the adversary] *by the blood of the Lamb, and by the word of their testimony.*[Rev.12:11] If you are tempted by the enemy to doubt your salvation or your standing before God, remember that *you have been redeemed through the precious blood of Christ as of a lamb without blemish and without spot.*[1Pet.1:18] And remember the scriptures that confirm your salvation. Make them *the word of your testimony.*

Now that you are re-born and re-created by the life of Jesus Christ, He is alive in you. This benediction is for you:

> *Now to him that is able to keep you from falling, and to present you faultless before the presence of his glory with exceeding joy, To the only wise God our Savior, be glory and majesty, dominion and power, both now and ever. Amen.*[Jude 24-25]

Chapter 17

Christic At Home In You

HAVING RECEIVED Christ, the kingdom of God is at work in the new you and in the new me.

We can never again negate, suppress or impugn the wonderful person that God has made of us.

We can never again condemn what God paid so much to redeem.

We can never again put down what God paid so much to lift up.

We can never again accuse or judge what God paid so much to forgive and to make righteous.

We can never again do anything to harm or weaken or destroy what God paid so much to heal, to restore and to save.

We can never again depreciate, discredit or disparage what God paid so much to dignify and to make royal.

We can never again criticize or denigrate what God esteems to be of such infinite value.

Having personally received Jesus Christ, we discover the real *Life* for which God created us.

The Lord inspired me with these lines:

The Re-Born ME

The me I see is Christ in me!
Now I can be all that I see.
For now I see a brand new me!
God's embassy is now in me.

All luxury, and discovery;
New melody – my jubilee!
I've found the key. So, I decree,
That the me I see is Christ in me!

When Christ lives in us, our new life is really His *Life* within us. Paul said, *Christ lives in me; and the life that I now live, I live by the faith of the Son of God, who loved me, and gave himself for me.*[Gal.2:20]

We learn to say to our Lord Jesus:

Here is my brain; *think* through it.
Here is my face; *glow* through it.
Here are my hands; *touch* through them.
Here are my feet; *walk* with them.

Here are my eyes; *see* through them.
Here are my ears; *listen* through them.
Here are my lips; *speak* through them.
Here is my heart; *love* through it.

We learn to practice the awareness of Jesus in our lives. We begin to say:

I am somebody.
God and me are partners.

We share the same life.
Nothing is too good for us.

Nothing can stop our success.
We have divine power within us.
We are conquerors.
We are royal and we are rich.

We say "Yes" to what we want to be.

We say "Yes" to our greatest vision.

We begin to *be* what we want to be, to *do* what we want to do, and to *have* what we want to have.

We are forgiven, cleansed, righteous, transformed, justified.

We are healed, restored, resilient, energetic.

We are happy, confident, fulfilled, productive.

We are prosperous, successful, blessed.

We stand in God's presence without the sense of fear, guilt, condemnation or inferiority.

We see God alive in us—His kingdom at work within us. We have become members of His royal family. We have identity with Him.

We are a chosen generation, a royal priesthood, an holy nation, a peculiar people; that we should show forth the praises of him who hath called us out of darkness into his marvelous light.[1Pet.2:9]

Part

V

PRAYER

∾

THE
BIBLICAL
APPROACH

THE FIFTH STEP to receive BIBLICAL HEALING is to ask the Lord to heal you according to His promises and to believe that He hears your prayer.

Chapter 18

God Hears Prayer

TO PRAY WITH faith does not mean to beg and to plead for blessings. If we have accepted Christ as our personal savior, then we are a child of God, and He is our Father. We are not beggars. The Father wants us to come to Him as any child comes to its parents—to come with confidence.

Since the Lord has promised to heal us, He *wants* to heal us. It is His pleasure to see us well, happy and strong, just as any parent desires the best for their child.

David says, *Like as a father pities his children, so the Lord pities them that fear him.*[Psa.103:13] No good parent enjoys seeing their child suffer. Neither does our Father enjoy seeing us suffer.

You and I are invited to *come boldly to the throne of grace.*[Heb.4:16]

Jesus said, *If we abide in him, and his words abide in us, we can ask what we will, and it shall be done unto us.*[Jn.15:7]

Jesus invites us to *ask, and it shall be given...for*

everyone that asks receives.[Mat.7:7-8] He also promises, *if we shall ask any thing in his name, he will do it.*[Jn.14:14]

The Father invites us: *Call to me, and I will answer you.*[Jer.33:3]

Believe That He Hears You

The Bible promises: *The eyes of the Lord are over the righteous, and his ears are open to their prayers.* [1Pet.3:12] When we pray, we can be confident that God hears our prayer.

John said, *This is the confidence that we have in him, that, if we ask any thing according to his will* [or according to His promise], *HE HEARS US.*[1Jn.5:14]

Then John adds, *If we **know** that he hears us, whatever we ask, we **know** that we have the petitions that we desired of him.*[1Jn.5:15]

If we did not first know His promises, and know that they are made to us personally, we might not believe when we pray that He hears us. But knowing that His promises are ours, we can have confidence that our prayer—asking Him to do what He promised to do—is heard and honored by Him.

Chapter 19

Asking And Receiving

THERE IS NO greater blessing in following Christ than to learn to pray and to receive His answer. God wants you and me, as His children, to come to Him with confidence that whatever we need or desire, we can ask Him for it in simple prayer and faith, and it will be done for us.

He made many promises — and they are for you and for me — personally:

Call to me, and I will answer you, and show you great and mighty things, which you know not.^{Jer.33:3}

This is God's invitation to prayer and His promise to answer.

Ask, and it shall be given you; seek, and you shall find; knock, and it shall be opened to you.^{Mat.7:7}

This is Christ's encouragement to prayer and His assurance that our prayers will be answered.

EVERYONE that asks receives.^{Mat.7:8}

His promise is that **every person** who prays to Him shall receive His response.

*They that seek find.*Mat.7:8

*To them that knock it shall be opened.*Mat.7:8

*EVERYONE that asks receives.*Mat.7:8

It is always God's will to answer prayer. He may answer, "Yes!" or "Yes, but…" or "Yes, and…"or "Yes, later!" But He will always respond to our prayers.

Why Some Do Not Pray

When people do not pray, it is usually because they have no hope of an answer.

Some say: "I could have faith if I had not prayed so often without seeming to receive an answer." Or they may say: "I had faith until I prayed so desperately for so-and-so, and the answer never came."

Others blame God for not answering their prayers, when they may not have prayed according to His word of promise for them.

People often harbor inner confusion—a bewildered attitude about prayer because the response that they anticipated from God has not been manifested. As they abandon hope of receiving what they ask for, they may abandon prayer altogether.

Their hopes for an answer have been shattered. They may continue a prayer ritual, but the exuberance or energy of their faith has dissipated.

When faith's light goes out, life and prayer become ritualistic. You walk alone, for God cannot keep company with skepticism and unbelief.

Fear and insecurity influence the life in which the flame of faith has been extinguished.

The Marvel of Prayer

> **One of the most marvelous communions any person can enjoy with the Lord is to pray and to receive His response of love.**

It is so wonderful, indeed, that those who have perhaps only received an answer to their prayers once in their lifetime, treasure that experience as long as they live.

An elder may dry his or her tears as they relate a crisis in which they called on God and their prayer was answered.

Our heavenly Father desires that we enjoy this blessing every day.

But we must efface the memory of unanswered prayers. A host of people have abandoned faith and hope for their future by harboring memories of prayers they may have prayed without seeing the response from God that they desired.

Others, by an act of their own will, wrote those memories off as bad accounts and began life anew. They succeeded. They found happiness and God's abundance, too.

Basis for Prayer

The foundation for answered prayer is to realize that the *only* reason you can receive a blessing from God is to know that Jesus died to provide the blessing that you desire.

Thousands of people pray but never stop to ponder if what they ask for is provided by the sacrificial death of Christ.

They want healing "because they have suffered so much," or "because they are good, and sincere," or "because they have been faithful to go to church," or for other similar reasons which are no basis for receiving BIBLICAL HEALING from Christ.

The only sure foundation on which to base your faith for BIBLICAL HEALING is: *Himself took our infirmities, and bare our sicknesses.*Mat.8:17 *Certainly he carried our diseases and suffered our pains...and with his stripes we are healed.*Isa.53:4-5 (Hebrew Literal)

To receive God's response to our prayers, we must trust entirely in the merits and mediation of Jesus Christ, based on His work of redemption.

Whatever we pray for, we need to know first of all that Christ died to provide it for us in His vicarious death on the cross.

In His death for you and for me, he provided every blessing that we can desire or require.

When we pray, we look first to the cross where the price was paid for the blessing that we seek.

Since Christ died to provide the blessing, it belongs to us and we can be certain that He wants us to have it. So we claim it boldly by faith.

Seven Needs Supplied

Human needs are sevenfold. (Seven is the perfect, complete number in holy scripture.) God reveals Himself by seven *redemptive* names, showing His sevenfold nature which imparts His sevenfold blessings to our lives when we receive Him. Christ's death paid for this sevenfold redemption. Everything we can require or desire is provided at the cross.

Although this may sound theologically complex to some, I share it here because of its significance to anyone who wants to understand Christ's work of redemption. According to the Scofield Reference Bible seven *redemptive* names of Jehovah are outlined.

1. God is our RIGHTEOUSNESS (Jehovah-*Tsidkenu*).[Jer.23:6]

2. God is our PEACE (Jehovah-*Shalom*).[Jdg.6:23-24]

3. God is our GUIDE or SHEPHERD (Jehovah-*Ra'ah*).[Psa.23:1]

4. God is our PHYSICIAN or HEALER (Jehovah-*Rapha*).Ex.15:26

5. God is our PROVIDER or SOURCE (Jehovah-*Jireh*).Gen.22:8

6. God is EVER PRESENT (Jehovah-*Shammah*). Eze. 48:35

7. God is our VICTORY (Jehovah-*Nissi*).Ex.17:15

These seven names express God's nature. Being *redemptive* names, they represent the redemptive blessings which Christ died to provide, and which God wills for His children to enjoy.

Redemptive blessings are those provided by Christ's vicarious ministry *on our behalf*, in His death, burial, resurrection and ascension. (Get my 392 page book, THE MESSAGE THAT WORKS, which expounds these seven *redemptive* blessings.) In *redemptive* provisions, there can be no exceptions. They are all for *whosoever*.

Why God Answers Prayer

We can have faith to receive the answers to our prayers when we know that *Christ died to provide what we are asking for.*

We do not pray to receive BIBLICAL HEALING because we have been good, or faithful to church, or because we have suffered, or because our family needs us, or even because we want to serve God.

There is only one basis for claiming health from

Him: Christ bore our diseases and suffered our pains and by His stripes our healing was provided freely.[Isa.53:4-5] He suffered our diseases, in our place, so that we can be well.

We are God's children. He provided our health by carrying away our diseases. Health, therefore, belongs to us. It is paid for and it is offered freely. We have a right to this blessing. It awaits our claim the same as an amount of money deposited to our account at the bank.

If It Is Paid For—It Is Ours

The fact that Christ died to provide our health makes it *un*-necessary for us to suffer sickness. It makes it unjust and illegal for Satan to inflict disease on our body. He has no right to impose on us what God laid on Jesus. That is why we resist the oppressor *steadfastly in the faith.*[1Pet.5:9] We claim our health because Christ bore our diseases.[Mat.8:17] We refuse to bear the curse of sickness since *Christ was made a curse for us.*[Gal.3:13]

We discover that our physical healing is integral to our redemption. Paul said, *that the life **also** of Jesus might be made manifest in our mortal flesh.*[2Cor. 4:11] We realize that Christ suffered so that we might enjoy physical health.

In Part III of this book, we elucidated the fact that sickness is of the devil.[Job2:7; Lu.13:11,16; Ac.10:38] It is a curse.[Deut.28:15-19,27-28,59-61; Gal.3:13] It is not natural. It is a killer. It resulted from the fall of humankind in the garden of Eden. It never came from God. Satan imposed it.

When God redeemed the human race from the fall, the salvation provided by Christ included deliverance from sin **and its effects,** part of which is sickness, disease and infirmity.

When Christ bore our sins and put them away, [1Pet.2:24] He also bore our sicknesses and put them away.[Isa.53:4-5] He redeemed us. He suffered in our stead. He set us free from the curse of sin **and its effects** by enduring the judgment that we deserved. [Rom.5:8; 6:6; 2Cor.5:21]

Christ carried our diseases and suffered our pains for us, so that *by His stripes we were healed.*[1Pet.2:24]

> **When He paid such a great price to provide the blessings that we need, no other argument is worthy of merit before Him in prayer.**

Christ Did it For US

It is vital that Christians understand the fact that when our Lord sacrificed His life in our name, on the cross, He did it *as our substitute.*

He did not die for Himself. He died for us.

He did not carry His own sin away because He had no sin. He put our sins away.

He did not conquer and triumph over Satan for Himself. He did it for you and for me.

He did not shed His blood so that He could be near to God. You and I are *made nigh by the blood of Christ.*Eph.2:13

He did not give Himself in His death on the cross to supply His own needs. He did it for you and for me so that we may enjoy all of the goodness and riches of God.

He did not have disease of His own. He took our diseases away and provided healing for us.

The cross is not heaven's triumph over Satan.

**It is our triumph over
The Destroyer — The Killer.**

Christ's Triumph—Our Victory

God did not need victory over Satan. We were the ones who had sinned. We needed redemption. In order for God to deal justly with Satan and to provide a just redemption for us, He gave His Son to suffer all of the punishment that we deserved. Jesus took the consequences of our sin on Himself, in our name.Isa.53:4-5

Then Christ arose triumphant, in our stead.Col.2:

12-13; 3:1-2 His victory was our victory. We are now redeemed. We are free from sin. We are liberated from the slavery of Satan. We have peace now. We are healed now.

When we approach God in prayer, we do not come as beggars. We come as His children.

To receive these blessings that Christ died to provide, we remember the cross and His suffering which paid for these *redemptive* provisions.

That is why I impress upon people:

> **The foundation for answered prayer is to realize that the *only* reason we can expect a blessing from God is because *Jesus died to provide that blessing.* Since it is provided in His death, *IT IS OURS.***

Chapter 20

Prayer For Healing

KNOWING WHERE sickness came from and understanding that it is not the will of our loving Father that we suffer physically, we can come to Him in prayer, confident that He will grant us BIBLICAL HEALING and other blessings that are provided for us through the sacrifice of Christ.

He says: *Call unto me, and I will answer you.*Jer.33:3

Ask, and you shall receive, that your joy may be full. Jn.16:24

*Every one that asks receives.*Mat.7:8

So I invite you to pray this:

Prayer

DEAR Heavenly Father: Thank You for the announcement that Your Son is the Lord, my healer. I am thankful that Your plan for my redemption includes physical healing.

Before I understood that suffering and pain resulted from the rebellion of Adam

and Eve, I presumed that there was no escape from the menace of disease in my life.

I now understand that sin is what resulted in the deterioration of humanity, including the diseases that destroy our bodies.

Why did You love us so much? There was nothing in our nature that merited Your favor. Now I understand that Jesus not only suffered the punishment of my sins, but that He also bore the consequences of my sinful nature.

Now I know that He took upon Himself my diseases and suffered my infirmities so that I can be completely healed.

DEAR Father, Jesus' physical body was tortured and beaten beyond recognition. *His visage was so marred more than any other man.*[Isa.52:14] His back was striped. When they beat Jesus, *they plowed His back: they made long their furrows.*[Psa.129:3] *He was bruised and torn.*[Isa.53:5] My sicknesses were laid on Jesus so that I could be free.

Now I respond to Your love. I receive the miracle *Life* of Jesus Christ by faith.

I understand that sickness as well as sin has the same evil source — Satan, the deceiver. I turn away from him with total resolution, and I welcome Your presence, peace and health into my life. When Jesus suffered my sicknesses, *by His stripes* [because He suffered them] *I was healed.*[Isa. 53:5; 1Pet.2:24]

The *Life* of Jesus Christ, which now abides in me, heals me of all sin and disease. I am saved. I am healed. I am free. No sin can dominate or condemn me, and no sickness has the right to invade my body which is now the temple of the Holy Spirit.

JESUS is my Lord. From today, I shall enjoy health, because He is my *Life*, my all. He is with me and in me now!

Thank You, Father. AMEN!

BIBLICAL HEALING

Part
VI

FAITH

❧

THE
BIBLICAL
ATTITUDE

THE SIXTH STEP to receive BIBLICAL HEALING is to believe when you pray that you have received what you asked for. This step, we call *faith*.

Chapter 21

Receive Your Healing

MANY PEOPLE PRAY for years for blessings which God has promised, but they will not believe that they have received the answer until they can feel and see it. This is not faith.

Faith means that you are convinced that what God has promised, and what you asked for, is yours; that you have received it even before you can see or feel it.

> **Biblical faith is based on God's promises alone.**

• It is here that our natural mind (our human logistics) and our spiritual faith engage their greatest conflicts.

• It is the struggle of our reason against what God's word says.

We pray for healing, but sometimes the answer is not manifested at once. We may still feel the pain or the fever. God's word declares that *by his stripes we are healed.*[Isa.53:5; 1Pet.2:24] Our reason argues that the disease is still present, but we refuse human logistics and we look only to the word of God. We do not give attention to what we see or feel, but only to what God says in His word — and we act according. This is *biblical* faith.

God's Promise—The Sure Foundation

The Bible says: *Attend to my words; incline your ear to my saying. Let them not depart from your eyes; keep them in the midst of your heart. For they are life to those that find them, and health to all their flesh.* Prov.4:20-22

In this bible passage, Solomon instructs us to keep our mind, our ears, our eyes and our heart occupied with God's promise alone. This allows no place for fear, unbelief or discouragement. When we do this, the Bible says that God's word will produce *health in all our flesh.*[Prov.4:22] *He sends His word and heals us.*[Psa.107:20]

God has equipped every person with five natural senses: hearing, tasting, smelling, feeling and seeing. These are physical senses that equip us for functioning in this natural world.

But *God has also dealt to every person the measure of faith.*[Rom.12:3]

Our five senses are natural and physical, but our faith is spiritual.

It is through our five senses that we gain knowledge in our world, but it is not through our senses that we know God. We know Him through our faith. *We walk by faith, not by sight.*2Cor.5:7

Many who pray for blessings from God do not believe they have received the answer until they feel or see the results manifested. They have not yet learned what faith is.

Three Attitudes

There are three attitudes with which people regard God's written word:

1.

They AGREE that the word of God is true. They see the word. They admire it and read it. They may memorize whole chapters of it and recite them. They love the Bible and respect its contents.

They say: "The biblical promises are true — but not in my case. I don't understand why I cannot receive the blessings promised, but I know the word is true. It is a wonderful book. I believe it."

But that is as far as they go; they never act on what the Bible says. Biblical promises are to them a dogma, a creed, a doctrine to be venerated.

2.

They BELIEVE the word of God when they SEE or FEEL its effects. We hear them say: "I never received healing when they prayed for me, but I believe I was blessed." Others say: "I FELT something when I prayed, so I believe God heard me." Still others may say, "Oh, I have prayed so often, but I never FEEL anything." They will believe only if they see or feel. This is never faith.

3.

They BELIEVE God's word and ACT upon His promises. These are the people who have biblical faith. You hear them say:

If God says it, then it is true.[Num.23:19; Josh.23:14; 1Kg. 8:56; Isa.38:7; 55:11; Eze.12:25; Mat.24:35; 1Pet.1:25]

If God's word says, *By his stripes I am healed,*[Isa. 53:5; 1Pet.2:24] then I am healed.

If God promises to *supply all my needs,*[Phil.4:19] then He is doing it.

If God says that He is *the strength of my life,*[Psa.27:1] then He is.

They always act accordingly. You will hear them say:

"God is what He says He is."

"I am what God's word says I am."

"I have what God says I have."

"I can do what God says I can do."

"God will do what His word says He will do."

They act on that premise, depending on the integrity of God's word. For them, *He watches over his word to perform it,*[Jer.1:12] to see that, as Solomon said, *There hath not failed one word of all of his good promise, which he has promised.*[1Kg.8:56]

Four Confessions

1) Some say, "I'll have the blessing some day."

2) Others ponder, "It's wonderful. I should have it, but I can't seem to receive it. I don't understand."

3) The realist says, "When I feel it and see it, I'll know that I have it."

4) But the believer with positive faith says, "I have it now. It is written. It is mine."

   • Biblical faith rests entirely on what the word of God says.

   • It is independent of our natural senses.

   • Faith is the reality of what the senses may register as non-existent.

   • There is a continual conflict between our senses and our faith.[Gal.5:16-17]

Walk by Faith—Not by the Senses

Our senses often repudiate God's word. They argue and contradict the Bible insisting that the blessing is not real because we cannot feel or see its manifestation.

But biblical faith calmly declares: It is written. God's word declares it, so it is true. I accept it.

To walk by faith means to give God's word the

preeminence over our physical senses and human logistics.2Cor.5:7

To walk by sight means to give our senses and our human logistics the preeminence over God's word.

Faith is God's way. It is contrary to the natural way. God says, *My thoughts are not your thoughts, neither are your ways my ways.*Isa.55:8

God's way is for us to keep our mind, our ears, our eyes and our heart occupied with His word while He brings to pass its manifestation.

The human way is to keep our mind on the disease, our ears tuned to human logic, our eyes on physical symptoms and our heart filled with fear and apprehension.

But God's order for making His words *health to all our flesh* is to give all of our attention to His word ONLY; to believe it and to confess it, even if physical symptoms may contradict what He says.

God's first call to you and to me, if we want to follow Him, is to *forsake our ways and our thoughts* Isa.55:7 because, as He says, *My thoughts are not your thoughts, neither are your ways my ways.*Isa.55:8

God *calls those things which **be not** as though they were.*Rom.4:17 He pronounced the blind man healed while he was still blind, *and he received his sight.* Lu.18:42 He declared the lepers cleansed while the disease was still apparent, and as they went away, they were healed.[Lu.17:12-19] At the tomb of Lazarus, Jesus prayed: *Father, I thank you that you have heard me.*[Jn.11:41] He said that while Lazarus was still dead. He knew that God had heard His prayer for Lazarus to be raised from the dead. That was faith.

Faith means that we believe God has already done what we asked Him to do, even before we see the results manifested. We believe this because we know we have asked for a blessing that is provided for us in the death of Jesus Christ. We believe that God has answered our prayer, not because we see the answer manifested, but because God's word declares that we will receive what we ask for in faith. In this way, we also *call those things which **be not** as though they were.*[Rom.4:17]

Exactly When to Believe

Jesus tells us exactly how to pray and receive the answer. Having provided all that we need, He says: *All things whatsoever you desire, **when you pray** [not after you pray but before any answer is manifested —**when** you pray], believe that you receive them, and you shall have them.*[Mk.11:24] This is a significant promise in the Bible concerning prayer and faith. Notice: ***When** you pray, believe that you receive.*

We must understand the sequence of prayer and faith. Most people reverse the order. They think it should be this way: Whatever you desire, pray for it, and when you see and feel it, then believe that you have received it.

This is the way of the natural person who says: "Seeing is believing."

But God reverses the natural order and says: "Believing is seeing."

David said, *I believed to see.*[Psa.27:13] He did not say, I had to see before I believed. And God said of him, *I have found David a man after my own heart, which shall fulfill all my will,*[Ac.13:22] proving that *without faith it is impossible to please God,*[Heb.11:6] but by faith we can *obtain a good report* before Him. [Heb.11:2]

Human logic asserts: If I cannot feel it or see it, I will not believe it. This is not God's way, and nowhere can this attitude be supported by the scriptures. Thomas said, *Except I shall see…I will not believe,*[Jn.20:25] and this attitude displeased Christ.[Jn. 20:29]

God's way is, *Believe that we receive it **when** we pray, and we shall have it.* His condition is to believe that He answers our prayers **when** we pray.

In praying for BIBLICAL HEALING, God authorizes us to consider our prayer answered. This is true when we pray for any blessing that He has promised and that Christ has provided in His sacrificial death.

> **When God's word is the *only* reason for believing that our prayer is answered, *that is faith.***

When Healing Begins

God has not promised to begin our healing until AFTER we believe that He has heard our prayer. We are to believe that our prayer is heard **when** we pray. *We know that we have the petitions that we desired of him,*[1Jn.5:15] not because we see or feel the answer, but because God is *faithful...who also will do it.*[1Th.5:24]

Three Witnesses

In the matter of physical healing from God, there are three witnesses:

1. THE WORD, which declares, *By his stripes we are healed.*[Isa.53:5; 1Pet.2:24]

2. THE PAIN, which may assert that the sickness is not healed.

3. THE SICK PERSON with biblical faith who declares, *By his stripes I am healed,* conforming his or her testimony with God's word.

- They refuse to retract what they have said.
- They declare in the face of contrary evidence, "I am healed because God says I am healed."
- They remember the scripture, *Hold fast the profession of your faith without wavering; (for God is faithful that promised.)*[Heb. 10:23]

The person with biblical faith maintains his or her confession of God's word that they are healed, and God makes it good because He says, *My covenant will I not break, nor alter the thing that is gone out of my lips.*^{Psa.89:34} He promises, *My word...shall not return to me void.*^{Isa.55:11}

And they overcame him [Satan] *by the blood of the Lamb, and by the word of their testimony.*^{Rev.12:11} In other words, they overcame the enemy, first, on the ground of being a child of God, redeemed through the blood of Christ, and second, by confessing the word of God in their testimony.

How to Triumph over Satan

Sometimes, after one has prayed for healing, Satan will tell them that they will never get well. That is the time to confess God's word, and to say, *It is written, I shall recover.*^{Mk.16:18} *The Lord shall raise me up.*^{Jas.5:15} The word of God in one's confession will always defeat the adversary.

When Satan tempted Christ in the wilderness all the devil heard was, *It is written. It is written. It is written.*^{Mat.4:4,7,10} Three times, Jesus gave him the same response. The result: *Then the devil left him and angels came and ministered to him.*^{Mat.4:11}

Christ's way of resisting and overcoming Satan was by confessing the written word. Since His way is best, let us imitate Him. Paul tells us: *Neither give place to the devil.*^{Eph.4:27} And James added: *Resist the devil, and he will flee from you.*^{Jas.4:7}

The Nature of Faith

Biblical faith in God's word:

- Is not believing what we see or feel.
- It is being so convinced of God's promises that we believe them despite contrary evidence.

Too many people have the wrong idea of the nature of faith. They think it means a vigorous exercise of the mind to grasp God's blessings. They say, "I have all the faith in the world, but I refuse to claim something that I cannot see or feel." But that is not the *biblical* concept of the nature of faith.

Biblical faith for BIBLICAL HEALING is exactly the same as biblical faith for salvation. The Bible teaches that we must believe that we are saved, and confess our salvation boldly, on the basis of God's promise alone, *before* we sense the joy of forgiveness. The joy comes as we believe and claim the gift of salvation by faith. We believe and publicly confess, on the authority of God's word alone, that we are saved. This is biblical faith for salvation.

This is also God's way to heal His children who suffer disease or pain—or to manifest any of His *redemptive* blessings provided for us in the death of Christ.

When a biblical believer prays for physical healing, he or she accepts their healing on the basis of God's promise alone, and without regard to physical senses. They claim their healing, confessing it boldly, and it becomes manifest—as promised by God's word.

A biblical believer does not doubt that God has healed them because symptoms may not disappear immediately. They are confident in God's promise, and they rejoice in His word until it is fulfilled in their lives.[1Kg.8:56]

This is God's way of bringing about the fulfillment of any promise He has made to us.

The Blessing of Knowing

John says: *This is the confidence that we have in him, that if we ask anything according to his will, he hears us; and if we know that he hears us, whatever we ask, we know that we have the petitions that we desired of him.*[1Jn.5:14-15]

Knowing that He always hears us when we ask according to His word, we know that we have the answer because we know that He will do what *He has promised to do.* That is praying with biblical faith, or as James calls it, *the prayer of faith.*[Jas.5:15] That is the *only* way to *believe when we pray* that we have received what we asked for.[Mk.11:24]

Part

VII

ACTION

&

THE
BIBLICAL
RESPONSE

THE SEVENTH STEP to receive BIBLICAL HEALING is to praise the Lord for the answer to your prayer and to act on His promise.

Chapter 22

Examples Of Biblical Faith

IF WE BELIEVE that God has answered our prayer and that we *have received* Mk.11:24 the blessing we have asked for, we automatically do two things:

1) We joyfully thank Him for the answer.

2) We put our faith into action.

Examples of Biblical Faith

• Abraham *gave glory to God* Rom.4:20 for the fulfillment of God's promise to him, long before the answer was manifested. He praised God because he was *strong in faith* Rom.4:20 and because he *believed* that it would be *according to that which was spoken* Rom.4:18 — [that] *which God had promised* [and which He believed] *God was able to perform.* Rom.4:21 He gave *glory to God* before there was any manifestation of what had been promised. He believed God's word. That was biblical faith.

• The Bible says that Jonah *sacrificed with the voice of thanksgiving,* Jona.2:9 for deliverance from the belly of the whale, even before it vomited him.

• Joshua and his people exclaimed praise to the Lord for delivering the city of Jericho into their hands even while the walls were still standing.[Josh. 6:10,16] They believed God's promise and praised Him for it while they acted their faith and marched around the city. As they praised and marched, *the walls fell down flat*[Josh.6:1-20] and the victory was theirs.

Not to rejoice in faith for the healing that we have prayed for and which God has promised and provided, would indicate that either we did not believe that we had received it, or that we were not thankful for it.

David says, *Let everything that has breath praise the Lord.*[Psa.150:6]

By him therefore let us offer the sacrifice of praise to God continually, that is, the fruit of our lips giving thanks to his name.[Heb.13:15]

Faith Proved by Action

Not only does biblical faith give thanks to God for the answer, but it is always accompanied by corresponding actions. James says, *I will show you by my actions what faith is.*[Jas.2:18] Biblical faith means that we are so convinced that God's promises are good, that we thank Him for their fulfillment and we act upon them, even before we see them fulfilled. And God makes them good.

We may take all the other six steps of faith to receive BIBLICAL HEALING from Christ, but if when we pray for healing, we do not believe that God hears us and that we have received the answer — if we do not believe that enough to act on His word of promise, then our faith profits us nothing.

Almost the entire second chapter of James deals with this vital secret of faith — *acting on God's word.*

What does it profit, though you say you have faith, and have not works [corresponding actions]*? Can faith save you?* [Jas.2:14]

If a brother or sister be naked, and destitute of daily food, and one of you say to them, Depart in peace, be warmed and filled; notwithstanding you give them not those things which are needful to the body; what does it profit? Even so faith, if it has no works, is dead, being alone. [Jas.2:15-17]

James here compares faith to love. He says that love in word only is of no value. Actions of love must accompany words of love. Even so faith in words is of no value if actions of faith do not validate those words.

God Said That I Am Healed

A lady who had a terminal sickness was sent home to spend her remaining time, and to die. She was a devoted Christian but had not been taught about BIBLICAL HEALING. One afternoon, she was reading her Bible where it says: *Who his own self bare our sins in his own body on the tree.* [1Pet.2:24]

She wept with gratitude because she knew that

Christ had already endured the judgment of her sins and they could never be punished again. She knew that she was saved and she was grateful that in the face of imminent death, there was *no condemnation*,[Rom.8:1] but only peace in her soul.

While rejoicing about this fact, she read further: *...by whose stripes you were healed.*[1Pet.2:24]

She re-read the first part of the verse. It was clear. Christ had already borne her sins. It was in the past, so she was saved. She knew it. No one could make her doubt it.

But what about these other words of the same verse, *By whose stripes you were healed?* Could they be as true as the part concerning her sins? "Yes," she reasoned. "They must be true. They are God's word."

"Mother," she called in a weak voice, "did you know that God says in His word that I was healed?"

"Why, dear, what do you mean?" the mother anxiously inquired.

"Look here," the daughter said, with tears in her eyes. "The Bible says, *Jesus bare our own sins in his body...so that we can live in righteousness.* Mother, we believe that. But look, it says more: *By whose stripes you were healed.* That means me. Look at it. *By whose stripes you were healed.* Mother, it has already been done. I'm healed. Get my clothes. I must get out of bed."

The mother tried to calm her daughter but to no avail. The girl reasoned: "Have you not taught us to believe the word of God? This is God's word; it is true, and I am healed. God does not lie."

She arose, dressed herself, began praising the Lord as she walked through the house, and was completely healed. In less than three weeks, she was normal in weight, and X-rays confirmed that her lungs were perfectly healed.

What happened? She had believed God's word enough to act on it. It was her actions which proved that she had faith. She could have lain in bed and died had she not acted on God's word, arisen by faith and claimed or embraced the blessing that He declared was hers.

Why Many Die Prematurely

Thousands of good people die prematurely, assuming that they believe the word of God. But their faith is never accompanied by corresponding actions. James says, *Faith by itself, if it is not accompanied by action, is dead.*[Jas.2:17NIV]

Often people say that they believe God's word is true. But at the same time, their actions do not correspond with their testimony. Their faith may be great, but the Bible calls it *dead faith that profits nothing*. There is no ACTION.

James said in substance: *Try to convince me that you have faith, when you never act like it; I will ask you to observe my actions to see my faith.*[Jas.2:18LT]

Take Me at My Word
—Arise—

Reverend Byrum, a great Bible teacher, relates the following incident from his life:

"Shortly after the Lord called me to work for Him, I learned a precious lesson about faith.

"There was much sickness in our community. Three of our family had been stricken with fever. I felt the disease taking hold of me and was soon overpowered by it.

"Lying in bed with a burning fever, and suffering excruciating pain, I began to pray. I told the Lord that He had called me to a ministry which I was unable to fulfill.

"There were no elders that I could call who believed in healing, so I began to pray to the Lord and to quote His promises, one of which was: *If you abide in me, and my words abide in you, you shall ask what you will, and it shall be done to you.* Jn.15:7

"I said, 'Lord, I am abiding in You; and Your words are abiding in me, so this promise is mine. I pray You, with all my heart, heal me.'

"Then I waited for the work to be done, but no change came. Finally I said, 'Lord, why am I not being healed?'

"The answer came at once: 'Take me at my word and arise.' I said, 'Amen, Lord, I will.' And without hesitation, I began to get out of bed. It seemed as if my head would burst with pain, but in my weakness, I began to dress myself.

"When half-dressed a slight change came over me, and dropping to my knees, I thanked the Lord. After dressing, I was much better. I walked into another room declaring that the Lord had healed me. Within twenty minutes, the fever had entirely left my body. I went to work, and was well from that hour.

"I am very sure that had I not acted on God's word, I would have had to pass through a long siege of sickness. It taught me a valuable lesson in trusting His word. I found that when faith is accompanied by action, in spite of every contradictory symptom, God will always fulfill His word."

James says, *As the body without the spirit is dead, so faith without works is dead also.* [Jas.2:26]

Action Is What Counts

All through the Bible, people of faith were people of action. Those who believed God's word were those who acted on His word.

• Jesus said to the paralytic: *Arise, and take up your bed, and go your way into your house.* [Mk.2:11] The man did not answer, "But Lord, I am paralyzed." He believed Christ's spoken word enough to act on it. His action proved his faith.

Immediately he arose, took up his bed, and went forth before them all. [Mk.2:12]

• Jesus commanded a man with a withered hand, *Stretch forth your hand.* [Mk.3:5] The man acted on the word of the Lord and was miraculously restored.

• At Peter's house, his mother-in-law was bedfast, sick of a fever. Jesus *rebuked the fever,*[Lu.4:39] [and Mark says], *He took her by the hand, and lifted her up; and immediately the fever left her.*[Mk.1:31] This is a perfect example of biblical faith in action:

1) He rebuked the fever.

2) He made her arise and act her faith.

3) The fever left her.

• In the book of Acts, Peter commanded the crippled man: *In the name of Jesus Christ of Nazareth, rise up and walk. And he took him by the right hand, and lifted him up: and immediately his feet and ankle bones received strength.*[Ac.3:6-7]

The man acted on the words of Peter, spoken in Jesus' name, and was miraculously healed. *He leaping up stood, and walked, and entered with them into the temple, walking, and leaping, and praising God.*[Ac.3:7-9]

• On another occasion, Peter told a man who had been paralyzed for eight years, *Aeneas, Jesus Christ makes you whole: arise, and make your bed. And he arose immediately.*[Ac.9:34]

Acting on God's Word

• We act on the word of our postman. He tells us that a registered parcel awaits us at the post office. We believe him and go claim the package, even before we have seen it.

• We act on the word of the doctor. He tells us to

take three pills per day. We believe him and take the pills, even before we feel the results.

• We act on the word of our banker. He notifies us that a friend has deposited a sum of money to our account. We can begin writing checks on the money, even though we have never seen it.

• We act on the word of our heavenly Father. He tells us, *I am the Lord that heals you;*[Ex.15:26] *By his stripes you were healed.*[1Pet.2:24] We believe Him, we go to Him in prayer claiming His healing. We believe that He hears our prayer. We arise from our bed of sickness and thank Him for the answer, even before we feel the results. We act on His word, and God confirms it. That is faith.

I watch over my word to perform it.[Jer.1:12LT]

There has not failed one word of all his good promise, which he promised.[1Kg.8:56]

All the promises of God in him are yea, and in him Amen.[2Cor.1:20]

Heaven and earth shall pass away, but my words shall not pass away.[Mat.24:35]

In the days of the Bible, people of faith acted on the *spoken* word of God. Today we act on the *written* word of God.

God says, *I am the Lord: I will speak, and the word that I shall speak shall come to pass...I say the word, and will perform it, saith the Lord God.*[Eze.12:25]

Daniel said, *And he* [God] *has confirmed his words, which he spoke.* Dan.9:12

Peter said, *The word of the Lord endures for ever.*
1Pet.1:25

Paul said, *The promise is sure to all the seed,* Rom.4:16 and *what he* [God] *promised, he is able to perform.*
Rom.4:21

The angel said, *No word from God is void of power.*
Lu.1:37RV

We are to believe God's word and demonstrate or validate our faith by putting our believing into actions that correspond. That is *biblical* faith.

Walk Out of Prison

Suppose a prisoner were to make an appeal for a pardon. The jailer comes and presents the document showing that the request for a pardon has been granted by a judge of the court. The normal thing for the prisoner to do is, 1) to be thankful, and 2) to walk out of prison because he or she is legally free.

Suppose the jailer reads the pardon, unlocks and opens the prison doors and says, "You are free to go."

But the person says: "I know the pardon says I am free to go, and I believe it, but I am a prisoner."

"The doors are open; come out," says the jailer.

"I know the doors are open, and I would be free if I were out; but I am not out of this prison."

"Well, come out," persists the jailer, and asks, "Don't you believe the pardon?"

"Yes, I believe every word of it, but it seems as if I will never get out of this place."

A pardon would be of no value to such a person, because they will not act on it.

It is the same way with the promises of healing. They are of no benefit to those who do not act upon them.

No matter how much we may pray—and even fast, if we do not act on God's word, our faith is dead and it profits us nothing.

No matter how many may pray the prayer of faith for us, our own unbelief renders those prayers ineffective if we fail to act on God's word.

Our hesitancy to act on His word is in reality our reluctance to accept God's provision. When we do not act on God's promise, it indicates that we do not believe we *have received* the answer. And God does not promise to begin our blessing until after we believe that we *have received* it.

Our acting on God's promise is what gives credibility to our *biblical* faith.

I Have Faith...But

Many people mentally assent that the word of God is true, but they do not act on His promise. Our *actions* are what express our faith; not our *words*.

When those four men, in the Gospel of Mark, came carrying that paralyzed man and let him down through the roof, Jesus, *seeing their faith* [not hearing them talk about their faith, but *seeing their faith*,] healed the man. He saw faith in their actions. Mk.2:5,11

We need never hesitate to believe God and to act upon His word. Jesus said to the father of the little girl who was reported to be dead, *Be not afraid, only believe.*Mk.5:36 He said, *The things which are humanly impossible are possible with God.*Lu.18:27 And the little girl was restored to life.

When God Speaks—Go For It

If God says, *I am the Lord that heals you* Ex.15:26 [and] *who heals all your diseases,*Psa.103:3 then we have the right to act upon those words, and God will make them good. We have His authority to rise up and take Him at His word, acting our faith, and He will confirm His word.

Our faith becomes stronger as we act on God's word. We become a *doer of the word,* Jas.1:22 a practicer of the word—not a talker about the word.

Since God says: *I am the Lord who heals you,*[Ex.15:26] and we believe His words, we act on what He says. That is when the bedridden arises by faith and is made whole. *The eyes of the blind shall be opened, and the ears of the deaf shall be unstopped. Then shall the lame man leap as an hart, and tongue of the dumb sing.*[Isa.35:5-6] Pains flee, darkness vanishes, and people begin to do the things they could not do before they took God at His word, acted on it, and were healed.

- Weakness is transformed into *strength.*
- Death is transformed into *life.*
- Sickness is transformed into *health.*
- Impossible is transformed into *possible.*

She Climbed the Wall

During one of our gospel crusades abroad, the crowds packed the great public hall from three o'clock in the afternoon. The gates of the wall that surrounded the auditorium had to be closed because the crowd overflowed into the compound and the pressure of the multitude threatened the safety of the people.

A man in the countryside had suffered a crippling paralytic stroke. His wife carried him on her back all the way from the country but, reaching the crusade venue, she found the big entry gates locked.

The poor woman was desperate to get her husband into the meeting for prayer. She saw others secretly climb the wall to get inside, so she decided to shove her husband over the wall. Then she crawled over it herself, picked him up and pressed her way into the building.

Following the message and the call for salvation, that dear woman carried her man to the platform for prayer. She was acting her faith.

I could see that they were desperate for a miracle from God. After earnestly praying for the dear man, I knew it was vital that he put his own faith into action.

I had an idea that was rather bizarre but I decided to do it. I steadied the man at the edge of the platform and told him, in the name of Jesus, to jump to the auditorium floor below (about one meter). He did it without hesitation, and the dear man was miraculously healed, and walked home with his wife that night.

> **Faith in action always wins!**

Chapter 23

The Next Step

W E HAVE NOW shared seven steps to receive BIBLICAL HEALING.

1. Know that the age of miracles has not passed, and that physical healing is part of Christ's ministry today.

2. Be aware of God's promises to heal in the Bible, and be thoroughly convinced that they are made for you, individually.

3. Realize that God wants His children to be well; that only Satan wants them to suffer disease.

4. Understand that BIBLICAL HEALING is a part of God's gift of salvation for you.

5. Ask God to heal you according to His promises and believe that He hears your prayer.

6. Believe when you pray that what you asked for has been received.

7. Give thanks to the Lord for His answer to prayer and act on His promises to express the validity of your faith in His word.

Three Basic Steps

These seven essentials of faith open the door for God to manifest in our life the blessings that Christ died to provide. He wills that we receive them. (Our book, THE GOOD LIFE, is a thorough study on God's seven provisions for our seven fundamental human needs.)

In essence, three steps are vital:

1. KNOW what God has promised.
2. ASK Him to do what He promised to do.
3. ACT like He did what He promised.

Knowledge of the promise comes first. Prayer is next. Action, with praise, is the finale.

When we have a clear knowledge of God's promise and have asked Him to fulfill it, then He expects us to begin to do, by faith, the things which we could not do without His help. Our actions and our praise prove the credibility of our faith, and God confirms His word, fulfilling His promises.

We rise above our doubts and fears to demonstrate our faith by our actions. We are liberated from Satan's enslavement. God's biblical promises are His guarantee of our freedom from sin and disease.

Act on What You Know

One night Christ's disciples toiled with their nets to catch a few fishes. But they had no success.

Jesus appeared on the shore and called to them: *Launch out into the deep, and let down your nets for a draught.*

Simon answered, Master, we have toiled all the night, and have taken nothing: nevertheless at your word I will let down the net.^{Lu.5:4-5}

Notice that he said: *Nevertheless, at your word, I will let down the net.*

Peter did not stop to argue the irrationality of his master's words. He did not stop to explain that he knew those waters and knew there were no fish in the area, he being smart enough to catch them if they were there.

He believed His Lord's words and put action with his faith. *And when they had done so, they inclosed a great multitude of fishes.*^{Lu.5:6}

There are times when we encounter people who have been ill for years. Doctors have shaken their heads in the despair of efforts to save their lives. Some have been told that only a higher power can heal them. Many prayers have been offered on their behalf but the answer has never seemed to be manifested.

I encourage such persons to fix their eyes on what God's word says: *With his stripes we are healed;*^{Isa. 53:5} — to let down their net *again.*

Peter said, "*Nevertheless at your word, I will let down the net.* The word of the Lord to us is, *Ye shall recover.*^{Mk.16:18} God's word cannot fail when we believe it and when we put corresponding actions with our faith.

A desperate father brought his lunatic son to Jesus to be healed. The Lord said,

> *If you can believe,*
> *all things are possible*
> *to them that believe.*^{Mk.9:23}

The father did believe and his son was healed. Jesus says those same words to every person who is in need of BIBLICAL HEALING right now.

Pray Like This:

HEAVENLY FATHER, I thank You that You have made known these truths to me. I thank You that Christ has borne my diseases and my weaknesses. I thank You that I do not need to bear them inasmuch as Christ took them in my place.

I understand that Satan is to blame for my sicknesses and that You have never placed a disease on me; You want me to be healed so that I can glorify and serve You by serving people. I thank You for the knowledge that Satan, *The Killer*, has no authority over my life now that I have Christ.

NOW FATHER, I come according to Your word, asking You to fulfill Your promise: *I am*

the Lord who heals you. I ask You to do it now, in Jesus' name, according to Your word.

I rebuke the enemy that has caused my suffering. In the name of Jesus, I command the life of my sickness to leave, and the symptoms to dissipate

Father, You have heard my prayer and have granted the answer. I claim healing according to Your promise. I thank You that the source of my sickness is destroyed, and that according to Jesus' promise, I shall recover.

From this moment, I shall put action with my believing. I understand that corresponding action is what makes my faith credible.

In Jesus' name I have prayed, and I know my petition is both heard and granted. AMEN!

Believe Your Prayer Is Heard

After having prayed that prayer and after having condemned the disease in Jesus' name, you can rest assured that God has heard and answered your prayer. His word says: *Hold fast the profession of faith without wavering, for he is faithful that promised.*^{Heb.} *10:23*

We allow the devil to hear nothing from our lips but the confession of God's word. If Satan suggests that God has not heard and answered us, we *resist him steadfast in the faith, and he will flee from us.*^{Jas.4:7; 1Pet.5:9} *He is a liar.*^{Jn.8:44} God's word is true. God watches over it *to perform it.*^{Jer.1:12; Eze.12:25}

We begin doing the things that we could not do before we prayed. We do them in Jesus' name, claiming the blessing that He has provided.

Reports constantly come to us from those who have been miraculously healed by our Lord as they have come to understand these truths and have acted on them. I would appreciate a personal letter from you telling me what God has done in your life as a result of this book.

Chapter 24

Four Vital Visions

I WAS BORN and raised on a farm near Pocassett, Oklahoma, the seventh son in a family of thirteen children.

At the age of twelve, my brother, recently converted, took me with him to a revival meeting in an old church down by the railroad tracks in Mannford, Oklahoma. I was dressed in my best country *overalls*. Since I could play the piano, I played for the singing. When the lady evangelist made the call for sinners to be saved that night, I was converted.

A Pivotal Experience In The Woods

From that time, I loved going to the little church. Oftentimes the work on the farm kept me in the field until too late to attend and sometimes I wept from disappointment.

At the age of fourteen, while bringing the milk cows from the woods to the barn, I began to weep without knowing why. I knelt by a large sandstone boulder to pray and had a pivotal spiritual experience. It was there that my heart was filled with a desire to become a preacher of the gospel.

At the age of fifteen, I left the farm to accompany a respected minister of our community, Rev. Ernest M. Dillard. Since I was musical and had an accordion, he wanted me to join him, with his guitar, providing music during the revival meetings. Each Friday evening, he insisted that I preach. So little by little, I found the words to express my feelings about Christ and His Gospels.

At 17, I Met Daisy Washburn

For two and one-half years, I accompanied Rev. Dillard through Arkansas and Oklahoma, and finally to California. In a little Church at Almo, California I met Daisy Marie Washburn who, with other young people from their Church in Los Banos, came to visit our revival. It was love at first sight for both of us, and one year later, we were married.

For two years Daisy and I traveled in California, conducting Church revivals. We were both musical so we played, sang and preached in many of the little churches in the agricultural San Joaquin valley.

On March 25, 1943, our daughter, Marie LaVonne, was born in the Bakersfield County Hospital. She lived only seven days. We were deeply grieved, but we determined to recompense our loss with spiritual births in the kingdom of God.

In the spring of 1944, we drove to Portland, Oregon to conduct gospel meetings in an old tabernacle-barn built and used by early Methodists. The meetings were successful so we founded the *Montavilla Tabernacle* Church and became the pastors.

While in Portland, on January 20, 1945 our son, Tommy Lee, Jr., was born.

We invited a missionary from India to speak at the church and were so impressed by India's need for the gospel that we decided to invest our lives in India as missionaries.

Our First Ministry Overseas

Three weeks after the birth of our son, we resigned as pastors of that growing church and began nine months of ministry across several states, in preparation for our five-year mission to India.

Trying to help the India people to believe on Christ, we were greatly disillusioned. We had invested everything we owned to go to the other side of the world to win souls, only to find that we could not convince the Hindus or the Muslims that Jesus Christ is the Son of God, that He has risen from the dead, or that He is alive today as the world's only Savior.

We had our Bible, but when we tried to convince the people about Christ by showing them scripture verses, Hindus had their *Sacred Vedas* and Muslims their *Holy Koran* which was considered to be God's word by the mouth of His prophet Mohammed.

Both the Koran and the Bible were black books, embossed in gold. Both were venerated as God's word. We could not give evidence that the Bible is God's word.

We did not understand about miracles. We could not persuade the people to receive Jesus Christ. We felt confused and demoralized.

Although a few were saved in our meetings, after a long siege of sickness during which our son almost died of cholera and I despaired of life for six long weeks with typhoid fever, in the fall of 1946 we returned to the United States and accepted the pastorate of a thriving Church in McMinnville, Oregon.

On March 13, 1947, we were blessed with the gift of our daughter, LaDonna Carol.

They Were Dead—We Were Alive

During our ministry at McMinnville, God dealt with us in many wonderful ways.

A lady in our Church informed Daisy and me of the death of the renowned Dr. Charles S. Price, a contemporary of Amie Semple McPherson. He was known for his miracle ministry across the nation. We had never met Dr. Price, but had taken a large collection of his monthly magazines, *Golden Grain,* with us to India and had read scores of his sermons and pictorial reports of his crusades. He was scheduled to minister during the annual convention of the Assemblies of God in Brooks, Oregon, only fifty miles from our Church.

Because of our disillusionment about India, we passionately anticipated that event. We knew that miracles were the answer to effective gospel ministry in non-Christian nations, but we lacked knowledge in that field, so we hoped to learn from Dr. Price's ministry.

With his demise, our world of hopes collapsed. I went to the Church, laid on my face and wept and prayed for hours. It seemed as though I could not contain my grief. The faith heroes and heroines of previous years began to pass before my mind like a panorama. I thought of Smith Wigglesworth, of Amiee McPherson, of Maria Woodworth-Etter, of E.W. Kenyon, of Dr. Price, and of others—not one of whom we had met or heard preach.

They were gone forever. The world would never again feel the impact of their miracle ministries. We would only talk of them and hear of their faith exploits.

As I wept, I wondered why this should affect me like it did. I had not met these people. I had only heard about their ministries.

I said, "Lord, those great heroes of faith are gone now, and millions are still dying. Multitudes are still sick and suffering. To whom will they now go for help. Who will stir our large cities and fill our large auditoriums with the magnetic power of God, healing the sick and casting out devils? What will this world do now?"

The Turning Point for Us

God responded to my spiritual search in a marvelous way, though not immediately. Within a few months, we received four visions that totally changed our lives.

We attended the camp meeting at Brooks, Oregon. The remarkable Rev. Hattie Hammond was chosen to minister in the place of Dr. Price.

She preached on the subject:

If You Ever See Jesus,
You Can Never Be the Same Again.

We walked out of that meeting in tears, and as we drove home, we discussed her message. I said, "Darling, maybe that is what we need. Maybe if we could see Jesus, our lives would be changed."

We loved Christ. We believed in the power of the Holy Spirit. We were respected in our organization as good and effective pastors, good evangelists.

We methodically prayed for the sick. But there were few if any results. Others applauded us, but we felt insecure in our lack of understanding miracles. We had gone to India to convince the non-Christians but we had been unable to cope with their ancient religions. We felt we had failed. We had been frustrated and discouraged. We thought that if we could see Jesus, as Rev. Hattie had preached, perhaps that would be the key.

The First Vision

The next morning at six o'clock, I was awakened by a vision of Jesus Christ as He walked into our room. I saw Him like I see anyone. No tongue can describe His splendor and beauty. No language can express the magnificence and power of His person.

I lay there as one that was dead, unable to move a finger or a toe, awestruck by His presence. Water poured from my eyes, though I was not conscious of weeping, so mighty was His presence.

Of all I had heard and read about Him, the half had not been told me. His hands were beautiful; they seemed to vibrate with creativity. His eyes were as streams of love pouring into my innermost being. His feet, standing amidst clouds of transparent glory, seemed to be as pillars of justice and integrity. His robe was white as the light. His presence, enhanced with love and power, drew me to Him.

After perhaps thirty minutes, I was able to get to the floor where I crawled into my little study room and lay on my face until the afternoon. When I came out of that room, I was a new man. Jesus had become the Master of my life. I knew the truth:

> **He is alive; He is more than a dead religion.**

My life was changed. I would never be the same. Old traditional values began to fade and I felt a new and increasing sense of reverence and serenity. Everything was different. I wanted to please *Him. That is all that has mattered since that unforgettable morning.*

The first vital vision had been revealed—

I had seen Jesus IN A VISION.

The Second Vision

In the month of September, 1947, we resigned the church in McMinnville and returned to Portland where we had been urged to resume the pastorate of Montavilla Tabernacle, the church that we had established before going to India. We expected to invest our lives in Portland, the beautiful *City of Roses.* But it was only to be a short step in God's design for our future global ministry.

Soon after that first vision, Rev. Gordon Lindsay brought the noted healing evangelist, William Branham, to Portland at the invitation of the ministerial association, to conduct a city-wide *Healing Campaign.*

We attended those meetings and witnessed hundreds of conversions to Christ. We saw amazing miracles of healing as Rev. Branham cast out devils and ministered to the sick in Jesus' name. The blind, deaf, dumb, and crippled were healed instantly.

I can never express the depth of my response to the operation of the gifts of healing and of the word of knowledge in that great meeting.

For three or four years, I had been deeply concerned about our traditional methods of praying for the sick and was distraught by the lack of miracles.

As we watched this evangelist minister to the sick, I was captivated by the healing of a deaf-mute girl, over whom he prayed a simple prayer.

In a quiet but authoritative voice, he spoke: "You deaf and dumb spirit, I adjure you in Jesus' name, leave the child." Then he snapped his fingers, and the girl heard and spoke perfectly.

When I witnessed that and many other miracles, a thousand voices seemed to whirl over my head, saying, *"You can do that! That's the Bible way! Peter and Paul did it that way! That's the way Jesus did it. That proves that the Bible way works today! You can do that! That's what God wants you to do!"*

We went home in total awe and reverent exuberance. *We had witnessed the Bible in action.* It was what I had longed to witness. At last, I had seen God do what He promised to do *through a human person*. Our lives were changed that night.

That was our second vision—

We saw Jesus IN A PERSON.

The Third Vision

Many days of fasting and prayer followed. Daisy and I determined to be channels through which the Lord would minister His healing love to our generation.

We sat down with our Bibles and talked about the wonders we had beheld. We reflected upon our disillusionment in India. We knew that the miracle ministry of Jesus was what would convince the non-Christian world about Him.

• We resolved to read the New Testament—especially the Gospels and the Acts of the Apostles, *as though we had never read them before.*

• Everything Jesus said He would do, *we would expect Him to do it.*

• Everything He said for us to do in His name, *we would do it.*

Days of intense reading of the teachings and ministry of Jesus Christ followed. The Bible, which had been little more than a religious book, was now a living, vibrant, message from God.

It was during this search that we discovered the dynamic and personal promises of Christ and the commitments He made to believers.

We saw the third vital vision—

We saw Jesus IN HIS WORD.

There was no question about it.

Jesus and His Word became one.

He was speaking to us personally through the written Gospels.

We were thrilled about seeing *Christ in His word.* We knew that what He had promised to do, He would do. And we were ready to do what He told His followers to do.

Christ's wonderful promises and commitments made to His disciples were made to us too. We were His followers—His disciples. *If you continue in my word, **then** are **you** my disciples indeed.*[Jn.8:31]

He had told His followers: *Into whatever city you enter, heal the sick that are there.*[Lu.10:8-9]

He gave them power against unclean spirits, to cast them out, and to heal all manner of sicknesses and all manner of diseases.[Mat. 10:1]

Jesus gave them power and authority over all devils, and to cure diseases.[Lu.9:1]

We knew that was for us, too.

Those followers *departed, and went through the towns, preaching the gospel, and healing everywhere.* Lu.9:6

That is what we would do.

Jesus said, *Fear not; believe only.* Lu.8:50

We were not afraid. We *did* believe. We were confident. We would do what Jesus told *us* to do. We knew He would do what He had committed Himself to do.

The Fourth Vision

Although I had these wonderful experiences, I still wanted the Lord to speak to me in some audible way. (I learned later that when He speaks through His word, *that is His voice.*)

In order to withdraw from people so that I could hear the voice of God, I announced to our church that I would speak to no one by phone or in person, until I had heard from God.

Daisy assumed the pastoral ministry while I went into an upstairs room alone, to remain until God spoke to me.

In the middle of the third day, the Lord dealt with me, clearly and distinctly, and resolved my questions about the death of so many heroes and heroines of faith and about the global need for the ministry of healing faith.

The Spirit of the Lord impressed me as I read the first chapter of Joshua: *"My son, as I was with Dowie, Woodworth-Etter, Lake, Wigglesworth, Ritchie, McPherson, Price, and others,* **so will I be with you.** *They are dead, but now it is time for you to arise, to go and do likewise. You cast out devils; you heal the sick; you raise the dead; you cleanse the lepers. Behold, I give you power over all the power of the enemy. Do not be afraid. Be strong. Be courageous. I am with you as I was with them. No evil power shall be able to stand before you all the days of your life as you get the people to believe My word. I used those people in their day, but this is your day. Now I desire to use you."*

We began to invite people to bring their sick, the diseased, crippled, blind, deaf and dumb people to our meetings. We taught the promises of Christ to heal, to save and to deliver *all* who had needs, and we began to pray for the sick and to cast out devils.

Needless to say, God confirmed with miracles His word that we proclaimed, because we had taken Him at His word. We acted on His word. If God said it, then it was so. If God promised to do it, then He would do it.

Marvelous miracles took place.

A woman's hip had been crushed in an accident. An incompetent doctor had not set the bones so the hip froze in a twisted position. The right leg was stiff and atrophied in a partially bent position obliging her to walk with crutches.

When we prayed, the bones cracked loud enough to hear, and her leg was healed. She paraded in the Church aisle while listening to a choir of angels for thirty minutes after her miracle.

They brought a girl who was born deaf and dumb. We drew her close to us as I placed my fingers in her ears. I only prayed a brief prayer:

"You deaf and dumb spirit, I charge you, in the name of Jesus Christ whom God has raised from the dead according to the scriptures, to leave this girl, and to enter her no more."

Then in the quiet hush that followed, I snapped my fingers behind her head and she jumped and looked. I quietly whispered words in each ear and she repeated them clearly. The evil spirit had gone. The girl was healed. It was like Bible days. Jesus was unchanged.

That was when we had our fourth vision.

We discovered Jesus AT WORK IN US.

Now we had seen the vision that God wanted people to see when He sent Jesus.

Jesus said, *Anyone who has seen me has seen the Father.*[Jn.14:9] Later He said, *As my Father has sent me, so I send you,*[Jn.20:21] and promised, *Lo, I am with you;* [Mat. 28:20] *I will dwell in you and walk in you.*[2Cor.6:16]

Jesus came and showed the Father to the world.

Now we show Jesus to the world. He is at work in the believer. We are His body. He is our life. He continues His ministry in and through us.

We had made the grand discovery. We had seen the greatest vision of all — *Jesus alive and at work IN US.*

That discovery was the key that unlocked our future global ministry to millions.

Within a few weeks, we resigned the Church in Portland in order to take the gospel of the kingdom to the ends of the earth for a witness among all nations and peoples.[Mat.24:14] That was the summer of 1948.

Unprecedented Ministry

As the latest edition of this book goes to press, I can witness that, for well over six decades in more than a hundred nations of the world, we have acted on the written word of God, preaching to multitudes of from 20,000 to over 300,000 people daily in mass gospel crusades.

My late wife and I (she passed away in 1995) have probably reached and led to Christ more *non*-Christians in *non*-Christian nations, and may have witnessed more great healing miracles than any couple who has yet lived — not because of any special faith, but simply because we began this global ministry so early in life and have ministered to so many multitudes, in so many nations, for so many years.

• We have been able to lead tens of thousands of previously unevangelized people to Jesus Christ.

• We have sponsored over thirty thousand national preachers as full time missionaries in areas, tribes and villages that had no gospel. Their new churches became self-supporting.

• Thousands of new churches have been established in previously unevangelized areas.

• We have seen deaf-mutes by the hundreds perfectly restored.

• We have seen great numbers of blind people instantly receive their sight.

• We have seen hopeless cripples restored — those in wheelchairs for as long as forty-two years — arise and walk. Those on cots and stretchers have arisen and have been made whole.

• We have seen crossed eyes go straight, stiff joints loosed in a moment, goiters and tumors disappear.

• We have witnessed eardrums, lungs, kidneys, ribs, and other parts of the body, which had been surgically removed, recreated and restored by God's creative power.

• We have seen incurables made well, cancers die and vanish, lepers cleansed, even the dead raised.

• In a single campaign which we have conducted, as many as 125 deaf-mutes, 90 totally blind, and hundreds of other equally miraculous healings have resulted.

• Conversions to Christ as Savior have numbered as many as 50,000 in one crusade, often many thousands in one night.

What we have seen our Lord accomplish in the past is an example of what He yearns to do in every nation under heaven, and in every epoch.

Our Gospel Is for All Nations

One of the most challenging statements in the Bible concerning the last days is in Matthew 24:14. Jesus said: *And this gospel of the kingdom shall be preached in all the world **for a witness** unto all nations; and then shall the end come.*

More literally in the original text,

Jesus said:

*This good news shall be proclaimed **with evidence** to all nations of the world, then shall the end come.*

This prophecy from the lips of Jesus foretells a great era of flaming miracle evangelism that proclaims Christ as Lord, *with evidence,* to the peoples and nations of the world.

From Calcutta to Calabar

From Alaska to Argentina, from Calcutta to Calabar, from Moscow to Manitoba, wherever we have proclaimed the gospel we have discovered one fact: *The masses gladly follow Christ when they can see Him confirm His word with signs and miracles.*

Whether the people are red, brown, yellow, black, or white; whether they are educated or illiterate; whether they are rich or poor, they all respond to Christ when they see His unchanging compassion in healing the sick.

Regardless of what religious academicians may teach, the undeniable fact remains that there is no substitute for the *demonstration of the Spirit and of power.*[1Cor.2:4]

Paul attributed the success of his ministry to the fact that God always confirmed his message with miracles.

The apostle *speaks of those things which Christ wrought by him, to make the Gentiles obedient, by word and deed, Through mighty signs and wonders, by the power of the Spirit of God; so that from Jerusalem, and* *round about unto Illyricum, he fully preached the gospel of Christ.*Rom.15:18-19

The writer of Hebrews says that Christ's *great salvation...was confirmed unto us by them that heard him; God bearing them witness, both with signs and wonders, and with divers miracles, and gifts of the Holy Ghost, according to his own will.*Heb.2:3-4

Chapter 25

Our Witness

THESE PAGES OF *Our Witness* are extracted from over a half-century of my personal journal. These are brief glimpses into what has taken place worldwide. Included are only *single days* of a *few* of the crusades which usually spanned ten days and often, two to five weeks.

To limit the size of this book, *dozens of cities* and entire *years* are not included. This is not a record of days when special miracles occurred, but of normal, ordinary days like ten or twenty or thirty other days of each crusade.

The Apostle John said of Jesus: *There are also many other things which Jesus did, the which, if they should be written every one, I suppose that even the world itself could not contain the books that should be written.* Jn.21:25   T.L. Osborn

February, 1949, Kingston, Jamaica: People gathered from early afternoon to get into the big auditorium. The crowds could hardly be controlled by the police.

We prayed for a throng of people out in the street, since there was no hope of their getting inside. Marvelous miracles were witnessed. Then we pressed our way inside and after preaching, several hundred accepted Christ. When we ministered to the sick, deaf mutes, paralytics, blind people, those with crossed eyes, goiters, tumors and all sorts of diseases were instantly healed tonight.

We prayed for a 17-year-old lad. At the age of 9, he had typhoid fever and it destroyed his hearing nerves and vocal cords, leaving him stone deaf and mute.

I placed my fingers in his ears and commanded: "You deaf and dumb spirit that was sent to destroy this lad's hearing and speech, I adjure you to leave him, in the name of Jesus Christ."

I *knew* that the spirit of deafness left the boy. He started to weep. I asked the musicians to play and he was simply ravished by the music.

The newspaper headlined his story and, as a result, the lad got a good job, went on to study music, became a top clarinet player and one of the excellent male voices in his choir. Hundreds believed on the Lord because of his miracle.

After praying for the sick for nearly two hours, I slipped out the back door, jumped over the wall and started to our car. An elderly woman grabbed me with desperation and asked, "You are Rev. Osborn, aren't you?" I replied, "Yes ma'am, I am."

"Oh please," she begged, "I am totally blind. I cannot even see the light. If you will touch my eyes, I will be healed. I know God will heal me."

Christ's compassion gripped my heart, and I knew He wanted to heal her.

There in the dark I laid my hands on her eyes and said, "Woman, in the name of Jesus Christ whom God raised from the dead, I command your blind eyes to be opened. Receive your sight."

She almost pushed my hands from her eyes as she began to look up. Suddenly she exclaimed, "Oh, thank God! Yes, I can see. I can see everything. The moon, the stars, my hands. Oh, thank God. I knew He would do it."

No words can express the joy that floods one's soul in such moments.

March, 1951, Ponce, Puerto Rico: As I began to preach, Daisy told me that Juan Santos was present. His is the most phenomenal miracle that we have witnessed here. He was healed the night I preached from Mark chapter two about the healing of the cripple. We called him to the platform and he talked for about thirty minutes.

He had been shot in the back, destroying his spinal column and the nerves below his waist. He was left paralyzed in both legs. For sixteen years, his legs were dead, and completely atrophied, drawn double—and stiff. One arm was partly paralyzed. The other shook constantly so that he could hardly feed himself.

To move about, he swung his body between his hands, his withered legs resting in the dirt between each swing. He was instantly healed and is now perfect. His testimony is known by thousands in Puerto Rico as an undeniable miracle of God's power.

When Mr. Santos finished his testimony, (which was more convincing than a thousand sermons), an old lady mounted the platform, anxious to tell what God did for her. She had been totally blind. She reported:

"Friends told me that a man was performing miracles. I decided to find my own way to that meeting. I went early so I could get near the platform. I purposed that if I could touch the evangelist's clothes, I would be healed.

"People were pressed around me. I reached out my hand at the edge of the platform while he was preaching about Jesus. I finally grabbed his trousers.

"My eyes were opened and I could see. I shouted, *'Hallelujah! I can see!'* It was a great miracle. Everywhere I go, I tell people about how God opened my blind eyes. I am so happy and thankful to God."

It was not the trouser legs that healed that woman's eyes, no more than it was the garment of Jesus that healed the woman in the Bible. It was the woman's faith. She set a time to believe for God to do the miracle she needed.

Hundreds accepted Christ as Savior tonight, then a man totally blind came to the platform to tell that he could now see "Very clear! Very clear!" A paralyzed man was restored and stomped his feet for joy. Many others were set free. The crowd rejoiced as miracle after miracle was reported for almost two hours. It has been this way every night of this crusade.

January, 1952, Camaguey, Cuba: Psalm 105:1 says: *Make known God's deeds among the people.* We are witnessing a glorious demonstration of God's miraculous power here in Camaguey, Cuba.

I can hear ringing in my ears the shouts of *"Allelujah!"* from the masses of people who pack the old baseball stadium and field. As we walk the streets, merchants are triumphant. Clerks in the banks and post office greet us with a *"Gloria a Dios!"* Waiters and cooks in the restaurants do the same.

Numbers of times I have listened as a policeman, a hotel employee, a street-car conductor, or a bus driver explains to some eager person that "Mr. Osborn is no healer. Only God is the healer. Listen to God's word. Believe His promises."

God is fulfilling His promises as we proclaim His good news to the multitudes. At the close of the service tonight, more than a thousand accepted Christ. Then we prayed for the sick in a general, mass prayer, since there was no way to pray individually for the people. Scores of miracles were reported.

A woman who had been totally blind came to show how she had been healed. A man testified at length, in perfect speech, whom at least one hundred persons in the audience knew to be a bad stutterer, and he was perfectly free.

A woman was exuberant when she found that her stiff knee was healed. Another whose neck had been stiff for many years discovered it was free. Three paralyzed men threw down their crutches and were healed. It seemed there was no end to the miracles.

We have already witnessed 21 glorious days of God's wonders here. Crowds of thousands have gathered twice daily, to hear the word of God, to surrender their lives to Christ, and to be healed of their diseases.

The sick and crippled have been brought to the meetings on bicycles, carts, wagons, jitneys, carriages, tongas, buses, cars, ambulances, in chairs, in wheel chairs, carried on back, on cots, in beds, led on foot, and every other conceivable manner. Buses have been chartered from all parts of Cuba. Sick people are being brought from opposite ends of the island.

From 1,000 to at least 5,000 persons, and more, have professed to accept Christ as Savior in every service — twice daily. No less than 50,000 persons have publicly claimed to receive Christ as savior. Miracles have been the talk of this city. When a restaurant man was asked if he knew about the campaign, he exclaimed, "I've heard of no less than a hundred miracles just today."

One man, blind from birth, was led to the meeting. As he came onto the crusade field, he fell to the ground, having seen the Lord in a vision. He lay there for some time, and those around him thought he died. Suddenly he regained consciousness, stood to his feet declaring, "I have seen the Lord, and now I can see. I was blind, but now I see." He could see to read. His eyes were perfect. The multitude was hysterical with joy when they heard this report.

Six deaf mutes were healed during the meeting tonight. One was fifty-five years of age, and had been born in this condition. One young man who was going to commit suicide was gloriously saved.

A lady who had a large cancerous growth in her left breast found it completely gone after prayer tonight.

Psalm 107:20 says, *God sent his word and healed them.* That is being demonstrated in every meeting here. *The gospel is the power of God to every one that believes.*

February, 1952, Punto Fijo, Venezuela: Here we have a large open field that is surrounded by a wall. The road is jammed all the way from town to the meeting place. There are hundreds of cars and dozens of buses. The meeting is thrilling, as over 2,000 have professed to accept Christ and have promised to join a church in the area.

The miracles have been amazing tonight. An old man who had been blind for many years was partly healed the other night, and tonight God finished the job; his eyes were completely healed tonight. He was so happy. Another old man totally blind for six years was healed tonight, too. It is impossible to record all details of the stories told to us. A girl who was born with badly crossed eyes was completely healed; her eyes are now straight and normal. A boy with one deaf ear was healed and can hear the ticking of a watch. Scores of others have been healed who could not possibly get to the platform to tell us about it.

March, 1952, San Jose, Costa Rica:

At least 2,500 accepted Christ as Savior after the message. Then we prayed for the sick, and it seemed like all heaven opened as miracle after miracle was reported for nearly two hours.

A boy, who was dying with tuberculosis of the spine and could not bend his back or even move his head, was healed. The mother was in tears as the boy walked normally. At least eight deaf-mutes were healed. The father of one of them was so happy that he was reeling to and fro, intoxicated with joy, his face bathed in tears, urging the people to look at his boy. We checked the lad every way, and he is healed.

A woman who has been blind for two years, was led to the service and received her sight. A woman was healed of a tumor. A businessman was healed of a big rupture. He had been to the hospitals, but received no help. Tonight he was healed. At least 200 more raised their hands in the audience, signifying that they too were healed. It was impossible for them to get through the pressed crowd to testify publicly. Words fail to describe the glory of this great meeting tonight. The presence of God filled the place.

Finally, we were able to rent the immense Bull Arena. Moving to the big stadium attracted national publicity, enormous crowds, and the dogmatic opposition of certain religious elements.

The press here is influenced by the ecclesiastic hierarchy and they have published injurious and false reports, representing us as charlatans and deceivers, urging the "faithful" not to attend and not to bring sick people who would simply be tricked and manipulated.

When we arrived at the national arena in the city center, the police had already locked the gates. But at least 10,000 people had already gotten inside and were seated.

The Chief of the National Guard dispatched a messenger to announce that the event was forbidden. Thirty official agents were on hand to prevent the public from entering.

The pressing crowd in the street became so agitated that the agents were forced to open the gates and the people poured into the stadium like a human river, ignoring the guards, filling every space available. The officials could do nothing but listen to the message and assist those who were being healed.

The main newspaper headlined: *Forbidden To Bring Sick People To The Osborn Meetings.* The article contained demeaning and defaming misrepresentations, but the public continued to fill the stadium to capacity, for each meeting we managed to conduct, and from 2,000 to 3,000 people accepted Christ in each service. But, unfortunately, the police and the National Guard finally deployed enough force to bring about the interdiction of the crusade.

Without doubt, the meetings we have witnessed here in San Jose, Costa Rica have been some of the most glorious that we have experienced in any nation. One night, I preached on *The Will Of God To Heal ALL.* Following that message, thousands of people prayed the prayer for salvation. Then we prayed for the sick in masse.

Following the healing prayer, there was great reverence. Suddenly, a child that had been crippled and unable to walk, was placed on the platform and he began to run. It seemed that heaven opened and God's healing virtue and power literally filled the arena.

In three minutes, there must have been seventy-five miracles wrought. Deaf ears were opened. Paralytics shouted for joy as they began hoisting their canes and crutches to demonstrate that they were healed. Some abandoned their wheel chairs. Children were healed.

Before we could calm the multitude, the platform was inundated with people who had been healed. For over an hour, the glory of God saturated the arena as His healing love made the people whole. On the platform, gospel ministers and pastors wept for joy and gratitude to God.

At least six or eight deaf-mutes were healed. A cripple mounted the steps of the platform, thrusting his crutches onto the platform floor. He was so thankful to be able to walk without them. Blind eyes were opened. Asthmatics could breathe freely. Hernias and tumors disappeared.

The eyes of a child had been turned back in its head and had never been normal. It was healed. Its eyes were perfect and its precious mother was crazy with joy. A man who had not walked in six years was healed. Friends had carried him to the meeting, and after the prayer, He was well.

An old woman with a tumor so large that she looked nine-months pregnant, was healed. During the prayer, the tumor simply disappeared. Her dress became loose. Her physician was in the stadium. He was so shocked by this miracle that he came to the podium to examine the woman himself. He said, "If I had not been her doctor, I never would have believed that such a thing could take place."

Another woman was healed of a large goiter that prevented her from bending her head forward. During the prayer, the goiter disappeared. Many who were present raised their hands to affirm that they knew her. There was great joy among the people.

A business man brought his twelve year old daughter. From her infancy, one of her legs did not develop properly. It measured ten centimeters shorter than the other. He believed that the girl would be healed. As they walked home, the girl complained to her father that there was intense burning in the bones of her leg. By the time they reached their house, the girls legs were the same length. They returned to show the multitude what God had done. Being a popular business man, this miracle astounded many.

Each day, more pressure was put on us to stop the meetings. The people were practically forcing their way into the arena each night. The newspapers continue to publish their defamatory reports, accusing us of deception and fraud.

Finally, the police received orders to stop the meeting under pretense of protecting the public from the foreign deception and religious chicanery.

The police took Daisy and me, with our children and our Puerto Rican interpreter, under command and put us under house-arrest, with soldiers who stood guard at our doors, day and night. One of the pastors was allowed to bring us food from the market. Finally we were informed that we could leave the country, and the police escorted us to the national airport and onto the airplane.

February, 1953, Guatemala City, Guatemala: After

the meeting last night, a woman who had been sitting in a car, crippled and unable to walk for over five years due to a broken back, continued praying and suddenly felt that she should walk. She got out of her car and discovered that she had been made whole. Many witnessed this miracle.

Thousands were present in the hot afternoon service. We are having two mass meetings daily and will be here for at least five weeks. What a change this kind of crusade makes on a nation. At least 2,500 accepted Christ in tears today. Then I prayed for all who were sick. The miracle power of God was present to heal.

The first woman to testify had walked with the aid of two crutches for 15 years. She was made whole and left her crutches. Then a lady of 18 years was healed of tuberculosis in her hip. She could not bend it, and had to walk with a crutch. She was completely restored and testified weeping. Then a young doctor came to the microphone to confirm her testimony, saying: "I know her; she was incurable. We treated her; she could not walk. It is true. We can only say that truly, God heals!"

A wealthy lady and her son came running, extremely excited. He fell into my arms, crying out. "Oh, Mr. Osborn, here's my mother; she has been deaf since my birth. She has never heard in 23 years. Now she is healed. She hears. Oh, God is so good." Many people knew her. She testified in tears of joy.

Next was a retired medical doctor who had not been able to walk for several years; he was completely restored. A woman who had a rupture for 20 years was healed. A policeman was healed. An older woman who was carried in arms to the meeting was made whole. A man who was brought in a wheelchair arose and walked, healed by God's power. A woman also was healed and left her wheelchair. Afterwards, over 1,000 people remained in the audience who declared that they were healed; but we did not have enough time to hear their testimonies.

February, 1954, Santiago, Chile: After four glorious weeks here in the capital city of Chile, conducting two mass-miracle meetings daily, we concluded the long crusade with a parade. It was the greatest evangelical demonstration in the history of Chile.

Scores of trucks, wagons, carts, and every kind of animal-drawn vehicle were taking their place. Over 600 musicians were there from the churches. There were over a thousand bicycles. A huge Salvation Army float was beautiful. A whole unit of police assisted. The parade filled a street extending over 35 blocks.

The headlines of the evening paper read: *300,000 Evangelicals March in Osborn Parade.* Then the entire center spread of the paper was a huge picture of the audience, together with other pictures and articles about the parade, stretching across both pages. The whole city is talking about Jesus, His miracles, and the celebrations of praise. To God be the glory!

July, 1954, Djakarta, Java, Indonesia: From 40,000 to 84,000 people and more have been jammed together on the Lapangan Bantang grounds in this capital city. Today, I preached on *The Gospel for Everyone*, stressing John 3:16 and Psalm 103:3. Thousands of people raised their hands, eager to accept Jesus Christ into their hearts.

When we prayed for the sick, Christ confirmed His word. A boy, who had been blind in both eyes, was wonderfully healed and could see everything. A woman, who had been blind in one eye for nine years, was healed. A Chinese woman, who had been crippled for twelve years and who could only hobble on two canes, was miraculously healed. A woman, who had been severely paralyzed on one side for eight years, was perfectly restored. She was so bad that her entire left side had become drawn and stiff. Every part of her body was healed. Another woman, who had been paralyzed on one side for nine years, was completely restored.

A great miracle took place on a little girl who had been the victim of a disease which had destroyed the strength and muscles in her body. Her little legs and hips were just skin and bones, limp and useless. (It was probably polio.) For over two years, the child had not taken a step. The father brought her and laid her in his rickshaw during our message, and she fell asleep. As I prayed for the sick, the father laid his hands on his child and prayed earnestly. The child awoke and cried out: "Papa, I'm healed!" She was instantly made whole.

Two lepers were cleansed; one had been a leper for five years and the other for twelve years. They promised to follow Christ.

September, 1954, Surabaja, Java, Indonesia: Tonight over 4,000 accepted Jesus as Savior after my message on *The Healing of Blind Bartimeaus.* Two totally blind women were healed and could see everything. One of them had been blind for twelve years. A lady totally deaf was healed. At least fifteen other totally deaf people were restored. A woman, who had been so ill with tuberculosis that she had no voice, was instantly healed, and her voice was restored.

A Muslim woman stood listening to the message. Then, suddenly, she saw a great ball of light appear behind me on the podium. It burst, and then a huge open hand appeared behind me with blood dripping from it. She believed on the Lord Jesus Christ and was both saved and healed.

Another person saw a great light cover the field of people and a huge cross appeared. Then two pierced and bleeding hands appeared so large that they covered the entire audience. Blood sprayed from them over the people. Everyone who was engulfed in the flowing blood appeared to be immediately healed and made whole. But others feared the blood and fled from it, dragging their poor, crippled, and diseased bodies in a frantic escape to destruction. Signs and wonders like these and others are causing tens of thousands to believe on Jesus Christ and to trust Him for salvation.

March, 1956, Bangkok, Thailand: As we arrived at the gate where the crusade was being conducted, I found my Thai interpreter talking to a woman who had been healed. For nine years she had tuberculosis of the spine and was bent double. She had suffered terribly. She has been attending the crusade and had accepted Christ as Savior. This morning when she got out of bed, she discovered that she had been perfectly healed. Oh, she was thrilled. Neighbors asked her: "What happened? What medicine did you take? Who healed you?" She told them how she had believed on Jesus and had been healed by Him. They said, "It is better that you remain bent down and die than to give up Buddhism." She answered them, "You have your heart; I have mine. I accepted Jesus and He healed me." All day she testified. She told how one of her neighbors, who was unable to raise her arm, had come and was healed, too.

After the message, hundreds received Christ as Savior. We then prayed for the sick. A little leper woman was healed. The leprosy had affected her hands until they were just rigid and numb clenched fists. Her feet were numb and stiff also. Ulcers had erupted on her legs and hands. She said: "I was alone. I had no job. My parents died with leprosy. No one would talk to me or come near me or visit with me. I was lonesome. But now I have a friend. I am not alone. Jesus loves me. He is not ashamed to come to my hut. He is not afraid of me. I am healed. I am clean. I will always follow Him."

Many others told of tremendous miracles. This crusade is a great time of apostolic ministry among the Buddhists, and Jesus Christ is giving proof that He is alive.

The director of a large Bible Institute in Hong Kong wrote us the following letter concerning our Thai crusade.

"We invited M. Tsoi to speak at our Bible Institute. He is an evangelist and has been ministering in Thailand for the last two years.

"Having just returned to Hong Kong, we asked him if he had any information about the Osborn Crusades in Thailand. He responded that he not only knew about them, but that he had attended the meetings. He recounted some very interesting things:

"'Marvelous healings and miracles have taken place in Thailand by the power of God during the Osborn Crusades.

"'I personally know of six lepers whose flesh has been completely restored after the Osborns prayed for them. At first, they said that the burning sensation in their flesh had stopped during the prayer. Then later, I saw them myself and witnessed that their leprous flesh has become as clean and healthy as that of a child. Every sign of their leprosy is completely gone.

"'I've heard of other lepers who have been healed during the Osborn meetings but these six cases are ones I have seen and talked with personally.'"

July, 1956, Kyoto, Japan: Here in this seat of Shintoism, a city of magnificent temples, we are seeing great throngs gather on an open field to hear the gospel.

After preaching the gospel to the people, hundreds of them accepted Christ. Then I prayed for the sick en masse. People literally ran to the podium to testify. The platform was filled in fifteen minutes. A man who had been blind, carrying a white cane, was healed so perfectly that he could even read the Bible to the audience. It was amazing. Seven deaf mutes were healed. It was tremendous to see them weep as they embraced each other.

I don't think we have ever seen people so emotional. A woman was healed of cancer and coughed it up during the meeting. She is well. Three or four were healed of tuberculosis. A woman, lying on a pallet, arose and was made whole. A boy with paralysis and epilepsy was restored instantly. A woman with one leg that had been paralyzed for several years was healed. A boy was healed of crossed eyes; they became perfectly straight. Another lad was healed of a rupture. It was gone. A man, whose finger was stiff because the leaders had been cut, is now perfect; and he was so excited to show how his hand is now normal. Many other great miracles took place, but I do not have the time to record them all. What a visitation of Jesus to the Shintoists of Japan.

January, 1957, Ibadan, Nigeria: This is the largest all-African city on the continent. I preached on *Why Jesus Came.* A vast company of people believed on Christ as Savior. Then we prayed for the sick.

First to testify was a man who had been blind for fifteen years. His eyes were totally healed. Next was a man who had been paralyzed and unable to walk for more than five years; he was whole. Then there was a woman who had hobbled about on two crutches. Her family had helped her to the crusade. She was healed and paraded back and forth, holding her crutches in the air.

A man, who had dragged his body on the ground with his hands for over thirty years, was made whole. He had tied old rubber pads on his knees to protect them, and he used blocks for his hands to help him move about. He had been a beggar in the streets, and he was a Muslim. He gave a powerful testimony saying: "If Jesus is dead, how could He heal me? You know me. I have accepted this Jesus because I know He is alive!"

Suddenly, a woman rushed up to testify. She had been a hunchback without hope. They said she was so disfigured, it looked like she was carrying a child on her back. She was made straight in a second. The people around her were frightened by the power of God as it straightened her back. She was so crippled that sometimes she scooted on the ground rather than try to stand up enough to walk. The woman was completely restored. How great God is!

August, 1958, Rennes, France: Thousands of Gypsies and their caravans formed a great parade and came singing and marching through the city to the campaign grounds.

A Muslim from Algeria came confessing that he wanted to accept Jesus Christ as his savior. He went to the microphone and gave public testimony of faith in Jesus Christ.

Then a man, who is a famous Gypsy nightclub singer, came and testified that he, too, had been gloriously saved tonight. His wife was by his side in tears. It was wonderful.

Many others came and testified. I was particularly impressed by two outstanding Gypsy violinists who had played in the Gypsy orchestra. One is an elderly gentleman, an excellent musician. In his youth, he played for President Woodrow Wilson. The other one is considered to be the best Gypsy violinist of our time. He has been converted also.

Only God knows the glory of this occasion today. Rennes, France, and the Gypsy communities of Europe will never be the same.

August, 1958, The Hague, Holland: This crusade is truly historic — the greatest crowds in Europe's history to receive the gospel face to face. Police claimed that from 120,000 to 150,000 were gathered on the Malieveld grounds tonight. There were at least a hundred policemen present. I do not know how many scores of Red Cross nurses and staff with stretchers, and trucks were on duty.

It seems unprecedented to me the way this nation is doing everything possible to assure the success of this great campaign. Tonight I preached on John 3:16, 17. Never have we seen a mass of people more attentive. Thousands accepted Jesus Christ as Savior and were born again when we invited them to decide for Christ.

Then we prayed for the great mass of people, and miracles of healing took place all across the huge Malieveld field. There is no way I could convey the glory of this meeting. A girl who was 90 percent blind was healed. A man, who had a severe back injury, a cancer on his nose, and a double rupture, was perfectly healed. The cancer simply vanished. No sign of it remained. His back was as free as a child's, and both ruptures disappeared.

A woman who had been in a wheelchair for 21 years was perfectly healed.

A lad removed his steel leg-braces which he had worn, having been paralyzed by polio. He walked back and forth on the platform to show that his legs were perfectly healed. A man on two crutches was marvelously healed and came across the platform, carrying his crutches. Another man, who could only walk with the aid of two canes, was healed. A woman in a wheelchair got up and was healed. A lady was healed of cancer of the breast. It was gone.

An older woman, totally blind, was brought to the crusade in a wheelchair. That dear lady was completely healed.

There were scores of other marvelous miracles; and, as usual, hundreds raised their hands in the audience, saying that they were healed but could not get to the platform. Holland can never forget this day and can never be the same again.

February, 1959, Lome, Togoland: Such power. Such conversions. Such miracles. Every day more and greater miracles are taking place.

Tonight I preached on *Acting Faith.* Four lepers claimed complete healing. Two of them had ulcers all over their hands and feet. Now they have dried up. One of them had the type of leprosy where his flesh burned like fire. Now his flesh never burns, and he feels well. The other was the painful type, and she is free of all pain.

An older lady who was totally blind for over five years was healed and could count the fingers of people in the audience. Then there was a girl who was carried by her father from a far-away village. For some years she had not walked a step. Tonight she could run and jump, like any girl.

A young man was carried by his father to the meeting from a distant area. He had been unable to walk for about six years. He had tried all of the native doctors and fetishes, but to no avail. Then he heard about the campaign, and his father carried him here. He was completely healed tonight and just smiled and wept and rejoiced as he testified.

Another young man was healed who had been bedfast for three years. From far away in his village, he heard that the Son of God had come down to earth and was healing the people.

He was dying of tuberculosis and had no voice. His parents put him on an old market-transport truck and gave the driver a pig to take him to the field where "the Son of God" was doing miracles. They felt that if he was not healed, he would die anyway. If he was healed, he could walk the 50 miles back to his village.

He was laid under a tree near the crusade field, where he remained for three days. Tonight he was healed. As he testified, his voice grew stronger. He was one of the happiest persons I have ever seen.

The Lord's mercy never fails. We are thankful that He has allowed us to be His instruments to bring the gospel to these dear people. Over fifty towns and villages have already sent invitations begging us to come and preach the gospel to them or send someone in our place.

One man testified whose right leg was smaller than the other. Now he is well, and the leg is normal. An older man was healed of total blindness. A young man was perfectly healed of a deaf ear. It is truly amazing what God is doing in this nation of Togo!

February, 1960, Lucknow, India: Fourteen years ago, Daisy and I left India in what seemed to be failure. We sought God for the answer; Jesus revealed Himself to us, and now I take up my pen to try to set down what our eyes have seen. Officials estimate 50,000 to 75,000 people present in every meeting we conduct here.

Right in front of the platform, not three feet from me, there stands an old Hindu holy man in a dirt-smeared robe. His long, squalid beard and his frizzled hair shrouds desperate inquiring eyes. Yellow paint is smeared on his forehead. Mixed mud and dust cover his face and hair. In his right hand is a large Neptune spear that he guards as his staff. What a joy to give out the powerful gospel message to people like this dear man, steeped in religion and knowing nothing about the living savior.

I preached on Mark 9:23, urging them to *only believe*. Thousands did believe; and when I finished my message, we called upon them to accept Christ. It looked as though everyone raised their hands to receive the Savior—a sea of hands, a tidal wave of response. As in the Bible, *multitudes were added to the Lord.*

When we prayed for the sick, we have seldom seen anything like it. Hundreds were miraculously healed and began trying to reach the platform to inform the public.

The first was an elderly Hindu man, carrying two crutches above his head. He was radiant. His long hair and beard were flowing. For five years he had been crippled. Now he paraded back and forth, so happy. By that time, another older man with a large red turban came bounding across the platform. He, too, was healed completely.

A man, whose foot and leg were crippled, was perfectly healed. He had walked on one side of his foot which was turned directly inward with the ankle twisted over. Both feet were perfectly healed and straight. He ran and jumped as the people glorified God. Those who knew him were astounded by such a wonder.

Two men who were blind found their way to the crusade together. Both were healed. Their eyes were so bright and clear that one could hardly believe they had been blind. Two brothers, totally blind, were healed tonight. It was a most wonderful sight to see them look at each other and touch each other's face in admiration. Then a girl was healed of blindness and could see everything. A 70-year-old woman, who had been nearly blind for seven years, was healed and could see clearly.

A most touching miracle took place. A little Hindu woman, clad in a dirty cloth, testified in tears. She would praise Jesus, then place her open palms together and bow to me in East Indian fashion. Then she would reverently touch my feet and repeat, again and again, her thanks. She had been a beggar and a disease had so drained her strength that she could no longer beg, so she had crawled into the wood to die. Her children and her husband were dead. She was left alone in life to beg.

She would cry and touch my feet to say how thankful she was that she was no longer in the bushes, sick and hungry. Now, Jesus was her friend, and she was healed. "Now," she said, "I have strength so I can beg again. Now I am not sick and weak anymore. I can talk loud enough to ask for alms and get some coins for some rice to eat."

How thankful we are to have come again to India. There were at least twenty blind people healed tonight. Fourteen years ago we left India because we were incapable of convincing the Hindus and Muslims that Jesus is the Son of God, risen from the dead and alive today. Now we have come in the power of the Holy Ghost and God is confirming His gospel with mighty signs and wonders.

February, 1963, Manila, Philippines: Tonight the multitude was vast. I preached on *Four Steps to Healing*, closing with great emphasis on the fact that salvation includes healing.

Then we prayed for the sick, and God confirmed His word. A man who had been deaf for over thirty years was healed. A woman who was deaf for ten years was healed completely. A child, healed of polio, took off a steel leg brace and orthopedic shoe and walked perfectly. A lady was healed of a large goiter. A woman with one leg two inches shorter than the other felt God's power go through her, and both legs are now equal. Another woman was healed of a goiter and a blood disease. It was an outstanding case.

A man carried both of his crutches above his head as he came to the platform and testified. He can walk as well as anyone. A man, who had a cancerous growth on the side of his neck the size of two fists, was perfectly healed. The huge growth simply disappeared. He walked back and forth, pounding the side of his neck, shouting: "Look. It's gone. It's gone. The cancer is gone." One of the pastors who knew the man grabbed me and, in tears, said, "He's staying in our church. We know how he was. The cancer is gone. It was as big as two fists and was an open, odorous sore. It's gone. It's amazing."

April, 1965, San Fernando, Trinidad: The entire city has been affected by the gospel. Upwards of 50,000 to 75,000 people, perhaps even 100,000, have poured onto the crusade grounds for each meeting during this glorious biblical event.

Tonight I emphasized Christ's substitutionary work for each one and stressed Romans 1:16 — that *the gospel is the power of God to everyone that believes.* When I finished the message and gave an invitation to accept Christ, at least 5,000 people received Him as Savior. Then we prayed for the sick, and there was an avalanche of miracles.

At the edge of the crowd, groups were running after different ones who had received miraculous healing. Before we knew it, the platform was being engulfed with people who wanted to testify of what God had done for them.

A young man was rubbing his eyes. His left eye had been badly crossed, and he was nearly blind. Tonight his blind, crossed eye was completely restored.

Then an old woman wanted to testify. For over three years her right eye had been totally blind. She was completely healed. A thirteen-year-old lad, who was born deaf, was healed. A little baby, born crippled, was brought in the arms of its mother. There was no sign of knees or of knee-caps. Both legs were rigid and drawn against its chest. Doctors forced the legs down and bound them in casts. The mother attended the crusade and believed for a miracle. The legs became normal. They cut the cast off of the child and its two legs and knees functioned perfectly. It was a creative miracle of God.

A dear man was healed of a paralytic stroke which had left him dumb and helpless. His wife had to feed and dress him. But in the meeting tonight he was completely restored.

A little boy, whose left eye was blind after being hit in the eye with a stone, was completely healed.

Another precious man was carried to the crusade on a bed because he was paralyzed and unable to move his legs. He was instantly healed.

There was a woman who had been deaf for 32 years. During the prayer, her ears seemed to pop open, and she could hear the faintest whisper. A beautiful lad about twelve years old was healed. One leg was twisted inward, and the foot was malformed. This lad asked God to heal him as we prayed for the mass of people. The club-foot was straightened out, and his leg that had been twisted was made perfect.

Perhaps the greatest miracle of all was the healing of Harold Khan, a Muslim lad. When he was only twelve years old, his right leg was badly injured so that it stopped growing. Due to his rapid, teen-age physical growth, that injured leg had become 5 ½ inches shorter than the other one and was much smaller in size. To make matters worse, his left leg was paralyzed. Harold had to walk with the aid of a special shoe for his dwarfed leg, elevated on a 5 ½ inch platform, and his left leg had to be supported by a large, clumsy, hip-to-shoe steel brace

Before we prayed for the sick, Harold listened to the message and believed that Jesus would heal him. As we were praying, he took off the elevated shoe from his right leg and the steel hip-to-shoe brace from his left leg and accepted Jesus Christ. Then this awesome miracle took place. His short leg became normal and his paralyzed leg was restored to life as the Lord passed his way and performed this amazing creative miracle.

Harold and his mother came weeping to the platform, carrying the steel brace and elevated shoe. It was incredible to behold. He walked back and forth on the platform, and both of his legs were perfectly equal. It absolutely astounded the multitude of people—and it astounded me because, looking at Harold's perfect legs, one could not see any way that he could have used these awkward orthopedic aids.

Truly Jesus Christ proved again, by this great miracle, that He is the Son of God, risen from the dead according to the scriptures. Harold's entire family accepted Jesus as Savior and Lord of their lives.

A woman, 105 years old and blind, was led to

the crusade. She received her sight. What a miracle of mercy. Truly there is nothing impossible for God.

February, 1969, Kinshasa, Zaire: I am at a loss for words to express the glory and wonder of what we are witnessing in this vast city. Great multitudes swarm onto the big military training field to hear the gospel night after night. After preaching tonight, thousands responded to accept Christ. There seems to be no one who refuses.

After the prayer for healing, an avalanche of people converged onto the platform, from both sides, ready to give public witness of the miracle they had received. The dumb and deaf, the blind, lame, crazy and sick were all healed. The people cried and laughed and rejoiced.

I thank God that we can be among these people. It is an extraordinary experience.

December, 1974, Benin City, Nigeria: This is an enormous crusade in this city whose history is so steeped in pagan culture and primitive superstition. There were 50,000 to 75,000 in attendance tonight, and it is like that night after night as we pour the gospel into these multitudes.

Tonight I preached on Romans 1:16, emphasizing that *The Gospel is the Power of God unto Salvation.*

The message was clearly grasped, and a great wave of reverence gripped the people as they repented of sins and received Jesus Christ.

The platform was flooded by people, pushing, crying and rejoicing, wanting to tell what God had done for them. A boy wept as he confessed that he was a thief. Now he says he will never steal again. A lad testified whose right heel had never touched the ground because his knee was bent; he had to walk on his tiptoe. He was perfectly healed. His leg became straight and his foot was flat on the floor. Then a boy came who had one leg quite a bit shorter than the other. He, too, was perfect and walked with a true, even stride. It amazed everyone.

A woman threw away two canes with which she had staggered along for seventeen years. Tonight she was restored and walked perfectly.

A man came carrying two heavy sticks. For years he had only been able to stagger along by bracing himself with these two canes. Now he tossed those heavy sticks away and walked as well as anyone. An old blind woman was healed. She could see everything and was so happy. A young woman with one blind eye was completely recovered. At least three deaf mutes were healed, and many who were deaf in one or both ears were restored.

It's impossible to tell how great God's presence and power have been manifested among these dear people. Day after day they come by the tens of thousands and receive Christ and His miracles of mercy, then go away to spread the good word among their people.

February, 1976, Uyo, Nigeria: The newspaper estimated that at least 200,000 were present. I preached on *The Healing Of The Leper.* Each time I emphasized a point, the multitude would break out clapping. We directed them in a prayer for salvation, accepting Jesus Christ and confessing faith in Him.

After a long period of prayer and thanksgiving, I began to announce to them that it was time to accept their healing by faith and to put their faith into action. Some most remarkable miracles took place. A handsome lad, about fifteen years old, had been deaf since he was two years old when he had a bad fever. Tonight he could hear a whisper.

A dear man had crawled on his hands and feet in a pitiful way. His knees had been stiff. It seems that a deadening, stiffening paralysis, mixed with perhaps arthritis, had crippled him. His hands had been twisted and gnarled. To show us how he had managed to move about, he bent over and walked across the platform on his feet and hands. Then he rose to his feet and raised both arms heavenward and praised the Lord in such a precious way that hundreds of us wept for joy.

The next one who testified was quite an old man who, for the past eight years, had only been able to move about by scooting on his haunches with his hands at his side. He showed us on the platform how he did it. Then the dear old man rose to his feet with full dignity and showed everyone how he can now walk upright, which he hadn't done for eight years.

Then a dear woman came forward crying: "Look at me. I was a leper. See my feet. Now I am healed. Look at me walk. My feet are healed. I can feel them. They are well. I am healed." She left, crying out: "I'm healed. My feet are healed. I can feel them. They are alive."

Then a man came who had been totally blind for several years. He was able to see everything. Next, a woman who had been blind came rejoicing because she could see clearly. She had been led to the crusade. Now she rejoiced as she pointed out all the people.

A dear mother brought her child that had been paralyzed by polio. She was crying and thanking God because the child was healed and could run and jump and walk perfectly. Then an older man, who had been a witch doctor, came up the steps. He was ashamed of the curses he had put on people and the deaths he had brought on through fear. Now he wanted to receive Jesus so that he would never be a witch doctor again.

Suddenly, a young man about twenty-five years old came forward. He had no hair. For eight years, he had been a raving maniac. It took four men to bring him and to control him during the meeting. He had been in the University of Lagos, studying medicine. Then one day he suddenly began to lose his mind and became totally insane. Tonight during the mass prayer, he began to be calm, his mind was restored. Another man on the platform verified his story. It was an awesome wonder of God. He was as normal as anyone could be.

A man came up the steps who had been a leper. He was overwhelmed that the deadness from his feet and hands was gone. He could open and close his hands well. Every finger was free.

A young man about twenty years of age came and said: "I was mad. I was crazy. But now, I am healed." We were all tempted to be a bit skeptical of his words. He looked so nice. We wondered if his story was true, so I asked for his name. He announced his name over the loudspeaker. Then I asked if anyone knew him. Suddenly, some hands were raised. I asked the people who knew him to come to the platform. A fellow came and said: "I know him. It's true. He was crazy, and we had to hold him at times. He has been like that for several years." He was restored by Christ. What mercy!

An old woman who had been crippled in her back for many years came to testify. She hadn't been able to stand upright, always walking in a bent over position, supporting her back by bracing her hands above her knees. Now she stood perfectly erect, reared back, forward, and sideways; then she waved her arms.

A man about forty years of age came to testify. He explained that for eleven years he had been crazy and possessed by demons. His story was so bizarre that we asked if anyone knew the man, and some fellows quickly responded to confirm what he was saying. They had to keep his feet and his hands in crude, village-made iron bands with chains. He was kept locked in a mud hut. He would fight and try to kill people. They could not go near him, so he had to be kept in heavy restraints.

Heavy callused scars encircled both his wrists and ankles. Friends had removed the iron bands when they saw that he was healed, and the dear man was normal.

Who could doubt the glory and mercy of God after witnessing such miracles, signs, and wonders? All across the crowd, hundreds of people raised their hands to signify that they were healed but could not get through the0 tightly packed multitude to testify.

December, 1977, Nakuru, Kenya: At the far edge of the multitude, a woman who was born blind and had never seen in her life was suddenly healed. As she began to see, she became frightened. She could see masses of people moving about and was horrified by them because she had never seen before. Her husband held her until they could help her overcome the shock of seeing for her first time. A leading Christian businessman witnessed it all.

Then another blind woman was sitting in a car at the edge of the multitude. Her husband was standing by the rear of the car. His wife had been totally blind. When the prayer was finished, the woman opened her eyes and her blindness was gone. She fell to the ground, weeping and crying in panic because she had never seen before.

Then over at one side of the multitude, one of our helpers called Ismael had been watching a boy with terribly crippled feet. He walked on the sides of his ankles with his feet twisted upward.

All of a sudden after the prayer, the boy's feet straightened out and he could stand on them. Both feet were perfectly healed and restored by a creative bone miracle.

The Finnish missionary here, with two of our interpreters, came to our room, almost out of breath. They said that over on Kolingen Street, the police are having to forcibly open a way through the crowd in the streets so the cars can pass. A four-year-old child, who was born totally blind, received sight last night and the street is jammed by people who are amazed.

Thousands and thousands were converted today. And there was great joy in the city. It was like Bible days when Philip preached in the city of Samaria.

After urging them to follow Jesus and to go to church, we instructed them about healing and prayed for them to be healed.

Then we asked them to put their faith into action—to begin to do what they could not do before the prayer. It seemed that the healing power of God exploded across the field and, in every section of the multitude, groups started running, following cripples who had been healed or who had taken off braces or tossed crutches aside and had begun to walk and run.

A lad burst up the ramp, carrying two crutches in one hand and two braces with shoes on them in the other. That dear lad was marvelously healed. Just as I was trying to calm the audience, a girl about fifteen years old bounded up the ramp, carrying two large braces. There I was with two crutches and four big braces and shoes trying to get the audience quieted down enough to explain these miracles. Then I saw them handing braces and crutches over the heads of the people, passing them toward the platform in four places at once.

They rushed a woman up the right ramp to the platform, carrying two crutches and one brace above her head. Then someone yelled, "Look here." A woman, whose eyes seemed wild with excitement, came yelling and crying, carrying two hip-to-foot braces with shoes on them. It was pandemonium everywhere as you could see people with crutches, canes, and braces, waving them in the air in no less than a dozen places at a time. Groups could be seen breaking out of the crowd, running, as someone near them was being healed.

✧✧✧

May, 1978, Monterrey, Mexico: So much is happening so fast in this historic crusade. Tens of thousands of people are talking about it. A group from Veracruz came by plane. One of them had been paralyzed and was unable to walk. He is up now, feels strong, and walks erect. He walked up to me as I was preaching and wanted to testify.

Another lady from Veracruz, dying of cancer, came by plane. She rented six seats of space for her hospital stretcher to be placed onboard. She has been healed and left her stretcher behind as she returned to show her people what God has done.

A woman from Saltillo, with a broken leg and a fractured disc in her spine, was perfectly restored. One man who had been paralyzed for 27 years, hobbling on a cane, was completely healed. Another man, paralyzed by an accident, 20 years ago, was healed. He said: "I came for a miracle, and I got it."

Today the meeting was formidable. I preached on the healing of Bartimaeus. I stressed the point that God still heals the blind today. I emphasized what an opportunity it is when Jesus passes our way—how Bartimaeus himself prayed; how he asked for mercy; and how Jesus heard his cry; how he was healed and how he followed Jesus in the way.

I never was able to finish my message. Four times I was interrupted by miracles taking place in the crowd. I heard a rustle or disturbance or rejoicing out in the crowd. Two steel leg braces were being hoisted in the air, and a group was surging through the crowd toward the platform. I lost control of the multitude and had to suspend my preaching and wait. Up the steps came a girl, walking steady and strong. This dear child's bones had been diseased so that they would crumble and break under the weight of her body. Now there she was, parading back and forth across the platform like any normal child. She was miraculously healed.

We finally restored order and resumed teaching. Within fifteen minutes, another big commotion broke out. Someone far out in front of me had been healed and was moving toward the platform. There was a steel brace being waved above the heads of the people. I simply had to stop my message again as they triumphantly marched up the steps. There was a boy about ten years old. His father was carrying a big steel brace that had been strapped from the lad's waist, up around his chest, to support his neck. The boy had a disease of the bones which had twisted his body and neck severely and only the brace could hold him straight. Now he was walking upright with both hands in the air, and his father was in tears. The lad was made whole.

Then another young fellow was healed. His mother was weeping. She said: "My son had meningitis when he was only three years old. He is ten now and has not walked since that attack. He has only lain in bed or sat in his chair." He walked as normal as any lad.

Then a lady came to testify who had not walked in twenty-five years. She had received a leaflet announcing the crusade, but did not want to know anything about such a meeting or about Protestants. Finally, she consented to be brought to the crusade tonight, and the family was so happy because she was healed. She was overwhelmed.

A young lady, who had fallen twice, rupturing a disc in her spine, was unable to stand or walk. But during the prayer, she got up and walked and was healed. She was so happy as she cried: "Look at me. Jesus has healed me."

One dear man's heart was healed. He was scheduled for surgery because he could not walk more than a few meters without gasping for breath. Now he had walked thirty blocks to attend this meeting and was well and breathing normally.

A woman, who for seven years had eaten almost nothing because of a cancerous tumor in her stomach, was brought to the meeting by her daughter and was healed. It was wonderful.

December, 1979, Nakuru, Kenya: Today is one of those historic never-to-be-forgotten crusade days. Thousands received the Lord in their hearts. I led them in a confession of faith until it was clear that they had understood and received Christ.

Among the first to mount the platform was a mother with her three children. They had all been born deaf. Each was healed and able to hear. What mercy from God.

Then a woman bounded across the platform, stomping her feet and waving her arms, carrying crutches above her head. She had been in a terrible accident. Many of her bones had been broken. She had been dragged to the side of the road and left for dead because they could only help those for whom there was some hope of survival. Hours later, someone heard her groan and realized life was still in her. So they put her on an old truck and hauled her to the hospital. But she was so near dead that her bones were never set.

By the time she was strong enough for bone surgery, they would have had to re-break the shoulder, rib, and pelvic bones to align her twisted body. Since she was a poor village woman, she was left to heal as she was. She had to walk with crutches. Her left arm was twisted and could not be raised. Her shoulders were deformed, as were her legs and pelvic area. But tonight Jesus came to her and she was miraculously healed. She walked back and forth across the platform, waving both crutches above her head, raising her left arm, weeping aloud, praising God for His mercy to her. It was marvelous. What a biblical miracle.

Following her was a man about twenty-two years of age who had been crippled by polio when he was a child. He was unable to walk without crutches, but was wonderfully healed tonight.

A dear woman who had never walked in her life was carried to the crusade in a bed by her friends. She was visited by the Lord tonight, and she got up and began to walk. The Finnish missionary knows her.

We never prayed at all for the sick tonight. The people just accepted Jesus Christ and understood that, when He comes in, sickness must leave. They believed; they put their faith into action; and according to their faith, it was done to them.

One of the greatest miracles tonight was a young man who had polio when he was a baby and was unable to walk. He tried crutches and canes, but fell and broke his weak legs so often that he finally gave up hope. To move about, he dragged himself backwards on his buttocks, with his hands.

He listened and received Jesus Christ in his heart and was wonderfully healed. He got up and walked alone, back and forth across the platform. He showed us how he had to scoot along on the ground, then he jumped up and paraded his new miracle. He preached a sermon as he testified for no less than fifteen minutes. I was astounded at his words.

Then a lad came, carrying a steel leg brace in one hand and a shoe in the other. Polio had left him lame but Jesus made him whole.

What an honor to be used of God, to be part of such a spiritual visitation to a nation.

January, 1980, Embu, Kenya: A multitude crowded onto the Moi Stadium grounds. I preached on *Faith, Hope and Love.* It was perhaps the largest crowd ever to assemble for a gospel meeting in this entire native province. After the preaching, and after thousands had accepted Christ as savior, we prayed for their healing and they began being healed everywhere.

I commanded cripples to raise their crutches and canes or to toss them aside and to walk in Jesus' name. They did as I said, and soon we could see groups or crowds moving in four or five directions at a time as cripples were healed and crowds followed them. It was a long time before I could gain the attention of the people and get those healed to come up to the platform to testify.

Different outbursts of praise and joy would break out as others began to be healed. While crutches were being raised here and there, all of a sudden a blind man mounted the steps. His eyes were open and he could see everything. Then an old man with crippled feet was healed. He jumped and stomped across the platform with tremendous joy. He was completely healed.

Then a mother came with her daughter who had been out of school for two years because she lost her eyesight and had to be led about. She had been taken to the hospital in Nairobi but nothing could be done for her. For eight years, she had no vision.

Now her sight was restored. She and her mother were weeping for joy.

There was a woman who had been bedfast for six years, unable to walk or to help herself. Carried there on a bed and laid where she could hear us, she had been healed. Her friends came up the steps with her, and we all marveled at her testimony. She was so thrilled because she could stand, and even talk.

An old man came who had suffered in his back and could not bend over, as he said, "even to eat, but now I can play like a child." He stooped, squatted, doubled, bent, jumped and ran to show how completely his back was healed.

An elderly woman came whose hips were so stiff that she had barely been able to walk. Also, she was nearly blind. For three weeks she had been lying at home. Now she could walk and jump and run and see clearly. Then an old mother told how that, though she lived very near, she had not been able to come to the crusade meetings because of lame feet and legs; so her friends had carried her to the grounds. She was healed and walked like a young girl and was so happy.

Another crippled man was healed. He took off his braces and threw down his crutches. But, instead of coming to the platform, he and those following him paraded out of the grounds and up the road by the market place to show the city what God had done.

There was no end to the wonders that God did in the lives of people tonight. It is overwhelming to hear and to see such marvels of God. One woman with shaking palsy was perfectly healed, and her hands are as steady as a child's. What a night. What wonders. God is being glorified.

September, 1988, Surabaya (Java, Indonesia): This crusade is even greater than the ones we conducted here in 1954. The crowds are enormous and the miracles spectacular. As news spreads across this nation, it's like it was in the book of Acts when *there came a multitude out of the cities round about to Jerusalem, bringing sick folks, and them which were vexed with unclean spirits: and they were healed everyone.*Ac.5:16

The roads leading to the enormous stadium field are so blocked by traffic that we could have arrived quicker if we had walked. People being carried on stretchers, hauled in pickups and cars, brought in vans and native betjas.

Rev. Liem, who interpreted for me during our crusades in 1954, said, "This great crusade is more magnificent than the ones you conducted before. You've brought the same message and the same power of the Holy Spirit is here to confirm God's word; but the crowds and miracles are greater than they were before".

Tonight I preached on the subject, *Good News for Java.* Thousands of people responded to accept

Jesus Christ. The compassion of Christ is at work among the people as they put their faith into action. The first one to testify tonight was a young man about 20 years old, carrying a cane. He had been paralyzed by a stroke and came from a long distance. He was instantly and perfectly healed, and ran back and forth across the big platform giving thanks to God. Then he threw his cane out across the audience and said he never wanted to see it again.

Many who were blind in one or both eyes, recovered their sight. Many deaf people recovered their hearing. There were dozens of sick and paralyzed people who received miracles of healing. Jesus visited this multitude and has healed and saved many hundreds of them.

When I asked how many had been healed but who had not been able to get to the platform to testify, arms were raised all across the field. I wish I could relate what we witness in these crusades but it is too much to tell or to remember. God is glorified and thousands are brought to Christ. This is what counts.

December, 1989, Port Moresby (Papua New Guinea): We arrived at the municipal stadium to find an enormous multitude of people on the stadium grounds. They had come like human rivers — at least 50,000 people.

When I finished the message, there was an avalanche of miracles. The platform wasn't very high so the people actually jumped onto the stage from all sides, full of joy and exuberance, rushing to tell the multitude about their miracle.

A woman had been paralyzed and was brought in a wheelchair. She got up from her chair, left it in the audience and came bounding up the steps of the platform to tell what God had done. She was completely healed. When I asked her where her wheelchair was, she said, "Oh I left it out there. I won't need it anymore".

A man came next. As he wiped tears, he said: "I haven't been able to walk without crutches, but now Jesus has healed me". I asked him where his crutches were and he responded, "Oh I threw them away. I don't want to see them anymore".

Many deaf people were healed tonight. A young lady who was very timid was healed of total deafness. Both ears were clear.

It was so touching to see how the people actually clamor to get to the platform to tell what God had done for them.

Until 11:30 at night, we listened to one miracle after another. What a wonderful gospel witness for Christ in Papua New Guinea.

A strong young man with an athletic physique, came in tears to show what God had done. He had been a warrior in the mountains of New Guinea and one of his knees had been wounded. Surgical measures were unsuccessful and his leg was left stiff and unable to carry his weight. He has been perfectly healed tonight and can jump and bend his leg normally.

An old woman who had suffered for years was totally healed tonight and she jumped and danced all over the platform.

Then an old villager with a heavy beard came forward in a very serious mode and informed us, with great politeness, that he had been healed of a paralytic stroke that had left him unable to walk or work. He was so grateful to God for loving him enough to heal him.

A woman who had been unable to walk for four years was completely restored. How she wept as she told the multitude of her miracle! Many children were healed of fevers and of sicknesses that disappeared. All kinds of sicknesses and diseases were healed tonight. Many had come from the hospital and were made whole. A man was healed of a broken leg. He simply cut the plaster cast from his leg and began to jump and run as though it had never been broken.

These people have such simple faith. What an honor to be able to experience God's presence and love manifested among them. Each miracle meeting seems greater than the one before. This nation is truly witnessing biblical days.

April, 1992, Hyderabad (India): Tonight I chose for my theme, *With God All Things Are Possible*. I read biblical passages about God, about His power, and about Jesus and His miracles. I shared with the people how Jesus ministered to the people and wrought miracles among them. After each case recounted from the Bible, I described a similar case that we have witnessed in our own crusades, in order to impress upon them that Christ is unchanged today.

After I finished the message and led the multitude in a prayer to accept Christ as Savior, then I instructed them about healing and prayed a mass prayer for the Lord to manifest His presence in touching and healing the sick. Officials estimated that there were around 300,000 people in the multitude. They refer to it as the largest Christian event ever experienced in Central India.

After praying for the people, then I asked those who had been healed to come to the platform to report their miracle publicly. It was extraordinary to see their response. All across the vast field, miracles were taking place. There were three or four steel braces, with shoes affixed to them, hoisted in the air above the people, at the same time. The people were rejoicing and crying out to God with joy and thanksgiving.

Different groups began pressing toward the platform to report their miracles, which created an avalanche of people around the platform steps. Some were healed of polio. Some were healed of paralysis, some had been crippled, others had removed their braces and hoisted their crutches and other aids. Some had come on crutches and were made whole.

As they jammed every space on the platform, a beautiful distinguished Hindu woman, dressed in an orange sari embroidered with gold and silver thread, wanted to speak. She was weeping so much that she could hardly express herself. She had been hit in the eye by a stone that had destroyed the eyeball and left her blind. Being a wealthy woman, she had gone to the greatest physicians but nothing could be done. The eye was destroyed.

She came to the crusade because she was curious. Seeing the distress of the poor people crowded around her and being a kind hearted woman, she was so overwhelmed by the needs of others that she forgot her own need and prayed to God, in the best way that she knew, begging Him to show mercy to the other people.

Then she was intrigued by how many people were coming to the platform to testify, and by the miracles they were reporting. Suddenly she noticed that she could see clearly and that was when she realized that her eyeball had been totally recreated by God. She pressed through the crowd to tell us what had happened and to show the multitude that if they would have faith in God, nothing was impossible. What a wonderful testimony for the glory of God.

There were simply hundreds and hundreds of people healed across that field. Night after night it has been the same way. There is no way that we can hear all of the testimonies, but it is clear that

God is visiting this great city and the people can never be the same.

February, 1994, Bogota (Colombia): Here we are witnessing one of the greatest victories we've ever experienced. The multitude that has converged upon this enormous park-terrain is simply immense.

I preached tonight on the three greatest ideas from God for Colombia. I read the scripture in 1 Corinthians 13:13. *Now abides faith, hope, love, these three; but the greatest of these is love.*

Then I said to them: 1) FAITH means that we believe in God. 2) HOPE means that we reach out to God. 3) LOVE means that we are valuable to God.

As I expounded these three concepts, it seemed to have a tremendous effect upon the people.

When I finished my message and gave the call for people to receive Jesus Christ, literally thousands of hands were raised to indicate that they wanted to become Christian believers. After the prayer for salvation, I instructed them in faith to be healed and led them in a mass prayer, asking God to heal them according to His promise. Following that prayer, I asked them to put their faith into action, and to begin to do what they could not do before.

All across the vast park field, demonstrations began to break out as people were miraculously healed and those around them began to rejoice for what they were witnessing. I have seldom seen a greater demonstration of the healing power of God in a multitude of people. Blind people, cripples, those carrying canes or crutches, children who were crippled or sick, older people who were infirm and had been brought on stretchers or wheelchairs, and all sorts of miracles took place to confirm that Jesus Christ is the same yesterday, today and forever.

In over 50 years of ministry among multitudes of people, I don't think I have ever witnessed anything comparable. All across the field, canes, crutches, wheelchairs, body casts, and braces were hoisted above the heads of the people as they rejoiced and gave praise to God for miracles.

I counted six wheelchairs, eight pairs of crutches, and 15 or 20 canes and crutches hoisted above the heads of the people *at one time* and I don't know how many other braces and casts were being raised in the air, at other times, to show how God had healed them.

Colombia can never forget what they have witnessed in this enormous crusade. They have certainly experienced something *better than religion*, more powerful *than a ritual*, more glorious *than a ceremony.*

Late tonight, long after we had returned to our hotel room, Pastor Torra came to our room to tell us that after we had left the platform, people continued to pour onto the platform for over an hour, reporting miracles by those who had been healed during the mass prayer. He said that he could hardly believe his eyes or his ears. Each day, we wonder what God has in store for the next meeting. He never fails to back up His word.

To God be the glory for what we are witnessing in Bogota, Colombia.

June - October 1996, Ten of the largest cities of Russia and ex-Soviet Republics: Following the demise of my beloved wife, Daisy, on May 27, 1995, our daughter LaDonna and I undertook the most strategic mission of our entire ministry. We resolved to minister for a full week in ten of the largest cities of the ex-Soviet Union. Thanks to a series of miracles we have been able to get translated and published 10 of our major books in the Russian language, five of mine and five by Dr. Daisy.

I received the $50,000 insurance money from her Life Insurance Policy. Instead of depositing it, I sent it straight to the publishing house in Minsk, Belarus, to be applied to the publication of our books in the Russian language. For the first edition, we printed about 22 tons of the books, and later we printed another 20 tons of them to be given to the new believers all across the ex-Soviet Union.

Nothing has ever given me greater satisfaction than to see these thousands of ex-Communists turn to the Lord Jesus Christ. In every city, the response has been the same. The auditoriums have been packed full and often, many have been unable to gain entrance.

Following the miracle meetings in Moscow, the capital, we went to Russia's ancient, historic capital of Saint Petersburg. The meetings and the miracles were outstanding.

Our next crusade was in Murmansk, the world's largest city above the Arctic Circle. It is Russia's northern naval base. God wrought special miracles among those tough, northern people.

From there, we went to Minsk, the capital of Belarus, then over two thousand miles east to Alma-Ata, the capital of Kazakhstan, and to Beshpek in Kirghizstan, both Moslem cities on the western border of China. Then we went north into the vast Oblast of Siberia, to the great cities of Perm and Novosibirsk. Thousands of lives are changed in each of these historic events.

From Siberia, we flew a thousand miles to the south for our next crusades in the extreme eastern city of Kharkhov, Ukraine, the nation's ancient capital.

Then we flew back north to Russia's capital of Moscow. All across this vast territory, we've looked into the eyes of people who have existed for over 70 years in a total spiritual void, with absolutely no knowledge of God and no freedom to worship Him or to pray to Him. This mission to these ex-Soviet Republics has surely been one of the most remarkable experiences that we have ever undertaken.

During the Kirghizstan crusade, someone presented a gift to me that is inestimable in value. Under the dictatorship of Stalin, Russian believers secretly translated parts of my book, *Healing the Sick*, and typed it on an old typewriter, making three carbon copies at a time.

One of those dim and torn copies has survived. That script had been sewn together with some old oil cloth for a cover, and had been passed secretly to the hands of many people who were sick and incurable, and they have been healed. A dear man brought that precious document to our meeting and presented it to me publicly.

Following the meeting where the book was presented to me, a big gentleman came to tell me that he is one of the people to whom the type script had been loaned. He had been bedfast for three years due to unsuccessful operations on his spine. As he read the manuscript in secret, he had been instantly healed. He wanted me to know what God had done for him through the truths that we had presented in that book.

In over 60 years of ministry and of miracles in more than 100 nations up until this time, I've never addressed people so eager to know the truth about God as these beautiful people in these ex-Soviet Republics. Every time we invite the unconverted to accept Christ, hundreds and hundreds of people press toward the platform and pack the space, praying in tears to receive Jesus as their Savior.

During our ministry in Moscow, people have converged on this meeting from 210 different cities of the ex-Soviet Union—from 13 ex-Soviet Republics. What a joy to place our 10 major books in the hands of each adult who attends these meetings. They will transport them into hundreds of villages and towns throughout the rural areas of these great republics.

A young pastor said to me:

"Five years ago we didn't know that there is a God. Now we've learned to know about Him and we've believed on Christ. We are telling others and they are being saved."

Then he added with a big smile,

"Now I have five churches, and a Bible school. Your books have solved our problem. We are young in the faith and didn't know what to teach the people, but now your books will become our Bible school courses. We thank you for coming and bringing us your books."

The fresh wind of the gospel is sweeping across these ex-Soviet Republics. A new kind of life and a new beginning with new miracle evidence of the living Christ is taking form in this generation.

✧✧✧

January 1997, Medellin (Colombia): This crusade is a very special event. The churches of the area have come together to assure the success of this mis-

sion. The pastoral committee has been able to obtain permission to use the immense *San Antonio
Park* located in the center of this metropolis of over
three million people.

Tonight the great paved park was jammed with
thousands of people. It's hard to imagine any gospel scene that could be more beautiful than what
we've witnessed here in the heart of this narcotic
trafficking headquarters city.

I preached on *The Unchanging Christ of the Bible.*
I emphasized the miracles that Jesus wrought during His earthly ministry and stressed the fact that
He wants to save people and to heal people today
exactly like in Bible days.

I emphasized the power of the word of God and
the secret of faith which is to believe His word,
and then to put corresponding actions with faith.

All of a sudden, while I was speaking, a wheelchair was raised above the multitude and a group
of people in that area started pushing toward the
platform to tell what had happened. I tried to calm
the crowd but it was clear that these people were
not going to wait for the sermon to be ended for a
formal prayer.

Suddenly there was another wheelchair raised
in the air and another group was headed toward
the podium, followed by a small woman who had
been healed while I was preaching and had gotten
up and was made whole. As both groups mounted
the steps with great rejoicing over the miracles,

there was no use to try to continue preaching. A little woman was running from one side of the platform to the other, with the crowd cheering and applauding, giving glory to God. It was a real biblical scene.

As I was ready to resume my sermon, another woman came bounding up the steps, followed by some men carrying her bed. She had been carried to the meeting, incapable of walking. Surgeons had tried to repair damage to her back from an accident, but it only made her worse. The family brought her to the meeting and she was miraculously healed. The crowd went wild with joy.

Watching these miracles take place, I finally turned to the multitude and challenged them to make a decision for Christ. It was one of the most beautiful events that we have witnessed to see that vast plaza of people with their hands raised, calling on God in repentance and in faith to receive Christ as their Savior and Lord.

Suddenly an old man came to the podium, completely healed of paralysis. They had carried him to the meeting because he had been unable to walk or to talk, but now he was able to talk, to walk, to raise his arms above his head, to bend his legs, and to do anything.

People were being healed all over the plaza. I think this meeting is one of the most remarkable that I have witnessed.

July - August 1997; Four great cities of Poland: For a long time Poland has been on my heart. During the 60's a British missionary in India who was our friend, wanted to go to Poland and minister to the people while still under Communist rule.

Missionary Harold Groves managed to win the good will of the authorities and of certain Baptist and Catholic leaders who welcomed him to their formal churches to speak and to show the docu-miracle films of our crusades that we provided for him to take into Poland.

Each trip that he made into Poland, we would provide a projector and more films, always telling him to leave them in the country with the preachers, so they could continue sowing the seed of the gospel.

Having made this investment for these many years in this great nation, when the Communist walls crumbled, I had a great desire to go to Poland, myself.

We took steps to translate and publish our 10 major books in the Polish language. Then we organized crusades in four of the largest cities — Szczecin, Wroclaw, Katowice, and in the capital city of Warsaw.

We spent a full week in each city teaching for two hours each morning and each evening, Monday through Friday. Then on Saturday and Sunday we conducted great public miracle rallies to demonstrate to the people what we had taught during the week.

The meetings have been wonderful and the Polish people are so responsive to the gospel. Only God knows what revolutionary changes are imminent in this nation, following these powerful weeks of strategic teaching, the public miracle rallies, all coupled with our 10 major books. The harvest here is ripe, and I feel it is one of the most significant missions that I've ever conducted.

The Polish people have been enslaved by Communism. They are searching for spiritual reality in their lives. The gospel preached *in demonstration of the spirit and of power,*[1Cor.2:4] like the apostle Paul did, will change these people and will precipitate a new spiritual beginning across this nation.

Here at Katowice, thousands of people have been attracted by the Good News that we have been proclaiming here on a large open-air sport field where tens of thousands of people can gather for our public miracle rallies. The extra-ordinary miracles that God has wrought here is showing to them that the Jesus of the Bible is unchanged today.

One man was astounded when his left arm that had been paralyzed and atrophied, became normal. He raised his hand, moved his arm, clenched his fist, and wept as he told the people about the miracle he had received. The multitude applauded wildly as they saw this wonder of God.

One after another flooded onto the platform after we had preached and led the multitude in a prayer of accepting Jesus Christ. Then we had prayed for the sick and instructed them how to put their faith into action.

It was overwhelming to watch those Polish people put their faith into action then come rushing to the platform to tell what God had done for them. They were so anxious to make it known to their people that God was truly alive.

Communist propaganda had insisted that God is a *myth* and that religion is an *opiate*, but today on this big open field, as well as in each of the cities here in Poland where we have been ministering, these beautiful Polish people are seeing for themselves that the Bible is as true today as it was in biblical days.

One man came up the steps who had not been able to walk for years. He was instantly healed. He threw his canes away and showed the people what a miracle he had received as he bent his legs, doubled his back, jumped up and down as high as he could, then ran from one side of the platform to the other. His miracle made a tremendous impression upon these Polish people.

A dear woman was weeping uncontrollably as she told the people that she had been suffering terrible pain in her head for seven months. The neurologist had offered her no help. Today she has been made free of all pain and is so grateful to God for her healing.

Another lady came forward who had not been able to raise her left arm and now she had received Jesus as her Savior, and her arm was perfectly healed.

Many who were deaf were healed. Blind people recovered their sight. One woman whose right leg was swollen and inflamed, was made perfectly whole. A young man who had been an asthmatic since his youth, was completely healed. He had almost died several times, but now he can breathe completely free.

A man who had suffered for years because of an injury to his spine, was made perfectly whole and he could bend and jump any way that he wanted to.

There were so many miracles not only here in Katowice, but in every city where we had been preaching the gospel to these beautiful Polish people. God is doing signs and wonders to help these people believe on Christ. Poland is seeing before her eyes these essential elements of biblical Christianity in action:

1) The love of God for each person.

2) The power of the word of God.

3) The miraculous presence of Christ among believers.

4) His call to people to be His witnesses.

5) The seed of the word of God that produces life.

Poland has been ravaged and pillaged by war on many occasions. Today a new future of life and love is being formed in their lives. Despite near total annihilation—more than once in their past, Poland is on the rise, this time with faith in God.

I am so thankful that God has allowed me to bring the gospel across this great nation, and to plant the seed of His word not only in these four major cities through preaching and teaching the gospel for a whole week, but also through our 10 major books that we are placing in the hands of every adult that attends each one of our meetings.

July, 2000, Kiev (Ukraine): This crusade is probably the most significant and historic that I have ever experienced. It is overwhelming to realize that this is the first mass miracle evangelism crusade ever allowed out on an open public terrain, in the history of the ex-Soviet Union.

After weeks of persuasion, the government has allowed us to go out on a big field alongside the river that flows through Kiev. This sets a new pace—a new example of religious liberty. It inspires fresh courage and faith for young preachers that are rising across Ukrainia and the other ex-Soviet Republics.

Miracle evangelism in the open air is going to sweep across Eurasia and I predict that China will inevitably be opened for the gospel. Because the Russian and Chinese governments were trying to form a communist alliance against America and the West, they obliged their people to learn each other's language. Tens of thousands of Russians speak Chinese and as many Chinese speak Russian. God's harvest is going to be reaped.

Since the walls of the ex-Soviet Union have crumbled, the gospel is spreading across the ex-Soviet Republics. Tens of thousands of people are being saved. Many of them will cross the Chinese border and win the Chinese to Christ.

The multi-layered ex-Communist government in Kiev argued that *religion belongs inside buildings, not in the open air,* so they wanted to keep our meetings indoors. I told them that we have no religion; that we are bringing the living Christ to the people, and since He always ministered to the multitudes out in the open air, that's what we want to do in Kiev. Finally with the help of some parliamentarians favorable to the gospel, we obtained the permits.

The crowds that are pouring onto this beautiful field are enormous. Hundreds of automobiles lined the roads leading to the field, and the main road is like a river of walking people that flows from the trains, trams and public transportation vehicles to the crusade field.

What a marvelous new beginning for the Ukraine. What tremendous repercussions will result from this apostolic crusade. Young pastors across the ex-Soviet Union are going to be imitating what we are doing here. Tonight I preached on the subject *Something Better than Religion.*

After I painted the vivid pictures of religions around the world, then I contrasted how it must have been to attend Jesus' meetings in Galilee. It was intriguing to them to hear orthodox religion in the Ukraine compared with the beautiful, miraculous ministry of Jesus as He taught the multitudes out on open fields, and healed their sick.

It made such a vivid comparison to them that they could easily imagine the difference, and could see the apostolic and biblical quality of our meetings there on their field, in their own epoch, in their own city, among their own people.

I related many cases in the Bible where Jesus came to people who were sick or diseased or crippled, or to the lepers, to the blind, to the insane, and how He healed them, saved them and gave them new beginnings.

Following each Bible case that I talked about, I related similar cases that we have witnessed in our meetings around the world. It made it possible to present the Bible record with great clarity and reality to the people. I keep reminding myself here that these are people who have never in their lives known about God or the Bible. What a privilege to share Christ with them.

It is wonderful to see how they receive the message, and how thousands of them respond in tears to accept Jesus Christ as their Savior and Lord.

When I instructed them in how to believe the

Lord for His healing power, I assured them that He wanted to become their personal healer. It was so easy to lead them in prayer, after which I encouraged them to put their faith into action, and they did it at once.

Across the field one could see people being healed. Small groups here and there begin to exhibit excitement and commotion in the crowd, as some cripple or some sick person suddenly receives their healing.

At one point I counted 30 or 40 canes, several pairs of crutches and four wheelchairs raised above the heads of the people in the multitude that crowded before the platform. Each of these, along with small groups that knew about each individual case, were pressing toward the platform to come and tell us what God had done.

Unless one is in a meeting like that, it is not easy to imagine the glory and the wonder and Christ's presence as He comes among them to heal their sick.

Here in Kiev, we could say what was written in the Bible: *The Lord worked with us confirming His word with signs following.*Mk.16:10

We could say that *Jesus of Nazareth has been approved of God* among the people of Kiev just like among the people of Jerusalem *by miracles and signs and wonders which God did in the presence of them all.*
Ac.2:22

It is impossible to relate the hundreds of testimonies that are given from the platform every night. It has been one of the most gratifying events that I've ever been a part of — most of all because we are aware that this is the first mass miracle evangelism crusade ever permitted in the ex-Soviet Union.

Thank God, we are sure that this historic, pacesetting, mass miracle gospel crusade will become the standard for evangelism all across these ex-soviet republics as young preachers reflect on how the gospel has been proclaimed and confirmed by Christ who is *the same yesterday today and forever.* Heb.13:8

NOW AFTER MORE than six decades of mass miracle evangelism we are continuing to witness the loving and healing Christ-life, as we journey from nation to nation carrying His GOOD NEWS to people. My daughter, Dr. LaDonna Osborn, is pressing into new and unreached areas with the Gospel of Christ. In every nation, in each city, during all of her public evangelism Festivals of Faith and Miracles, tens of thousands of people accept Christ as Savior and thousands of men and women experience the healing power of Jesus Christ. The healing life of Jesus works through her just as it works through me. Why? Because Jesus is the same in women as He is in men.

In more than 100 nations, we are on the go, proclaiming and demonstrating the resurrection life of Jesus Christ, available to all who believe on Him.

AS THIS EDITION of BIBLICAL HEALING goes to press, *Jesus Christ* [is still] *the same, yesterday, and today, and forever.*Heb.13:8 What *He began both to do and teach* Ac.1:1 throughout Galilee, He *continues to do and teach* through believers in this 21st century.

In each nation where we have ministered, *Great multitudes have followed* [Jesus], *because they saw his miracles which he did on them that were diseased.*Jn.6:2

With great power [we have given] *witness of the resurrection of the Lord Jesus: and great grace* [has been] *upon* [us] *all.* Ac.4:32

Many signs and wonders [have been] *wrought among the people; And believers* [have been] *the more added to the Lord, multitudes of both men and women.* Ac.5:12,14

God also bearing [us] *witness, both with signs and wonders, and with divers miracles, and gifts of the Holy Ghost.*Heb.2:4

Chapter 26

Biblical View Of
The Osborns' Global Ministry

> This chapter documents the glorious finale of this book on BIBLICAL HEALING. A unique compendium of 324 Bible verses have been catalogued, abridged, paraphrased, personalized and merged to express the *Healing Ministry of Jesus Christ* in our modern epoch of time.

THE **BEGINNING** OF *the gospel of Jesus Christ, the Son of God,* [was] *written in the prophets.*Mk.1:1-2 Then this *great salvation, at first spoken by the Lord,* **was confirmed to US by them that heard him,** *God also bearing* **them** *witness with signs and wonders.*Heb. 2:3-4

Forasmuch as many have taken in hand to set forth a declaration of those things which [**they** saw — those] *who were eyewitnesses and ministers of the word; it seemed good* **to me also,** *to write*Lu.1:1-3 what we have witnessed and experienced *concerning Jesus of Nazareth, mighty in* **deed** *and* **word** *before God and all the people.*Lu.24:19

*We **bear record** of the word of God, and of the testimony of Jesus Christ, and of the things that we have seen.*[Rev1:2]

We are disciples which testify of these things and have written these things: and we know that our testimony is true.[Jn.21:24]

We Declare Our Gospel

*That which was from the beginning [of our ministry], which **WE** have **heard**, which **WE** have **seen** with **OUR eyes**, which **WE** have **looked** upon, and **OUR hands have handled**, of the Word of life; **declare we to you.** And these things we write to you, that your joy may be full*[1Jn.1:1,3-4] because **we declare to you glad tidings**, *how that the promise made to our fathers, God has **fulfilled the same** to US their children.*[Ac.13:32-33]

We have **re-lived Bible days in OUR generation.** Bible parallels for what WE have witnessed are abundant. Therefore this compendium of 324 scriptures is the best possible narrative to include in this book.

This arrangement of scriptures is **OUR** witness of Jesus Christ. It is **OUR gospel.** Our account is **contemporary**; but the facts of Christ are **UNchanged.**

God said: *I am the Lord, **I change not**.*[Mal.3:7] *I AM THAT I AM. This is my name forever, and this is my memorial to all generations.*[Ex.3:14-15]

We know of a surety that *God is **not slack** concerning His promises*[2Pet.3:9] to those who believe them **today.**

Jesus Christ is the same yesterday, and today, and forever,[Heb.13:8] **as WE allow Him to be the same IN and THROUGH us.**

Our Witness

We have witnessed that *all that Jesus **began** both to do and teach until the day in which he was taken up,*[Ac.1:1-2] and all that the apostles **continued** to do in the book of Acts, **is still God's will today.**

I am convinced that ***all** the promises of God in him are yes and amen,*[2Cor.1:20] and that they are indeed given *to **you,** and to **your children**, and to **all** that are afar off, even **as many** as the Lord our God shall call.*[Ac.2:39]

As He Is, So Are We

Christ became a human being and lived here on earth among us.[Jn.1:14LB] The angel told Mary, *he shall be called **"Emmanuel"** (meaning **"God is with us"**).*[Mat.1:23LB] *God was **in Christ**, reconciling the world to himself.*[2Cor.5:19]

*Jesus came **preaching the gospel of the kingdom** of God,*[Mk.1:14] and He told his followers to *go to all the world and **preach the gospel** to every creature*[Mk.16:15] saying, *the **kingdom** of heaven is at hand.*[Mat.10:7]

We are ***ambassadors** for Christ*[2Cor.5:20] because

Jesus said, *as my Father has sent **me** to the world,* ***even so have I also sent you** to the world.* Jn.20:21; 17:18

So we say, today: ***As he is, so are we*** *now in this world;* 1Jn.4:17 *we are **laborers together** with God,*1Cor.3:9 *and his divine power has given to us all things that pertain to life and godliness, through the knowledge of him who has called us,* [and He has] *given to us exceeding great and precious promises: that by these we might be **partakers of the divine nature.*** 2Pet.3:4

Messengers of the Gospel

*The glorious **gospel** of the blessed God, has been* **committed to our trust,**1Tim.1:11 *that Christ Jesus came into the world to save **sinners**.*1Tim.1:15

*For Christ's death on the cross has made peace with God **for us all** by his Word.*Col.1:20LB *He has **brought us back as his friends**, and has done this through the death on the cross of his own human body, and now as a result, we are standing before God with **nothing left against us**, the only condition being **that we fully believe the Truth, convinced of the Good News** that Jesus died for us.*Col.1:21-23LB

*So everywhere we go, **we talk about Christ** to all who will listen… **This is our work**, and we can do it only because **Christ's mighty energy** is at work within us.*Col.1:28-29LB

We are messengers and *servants of Jesus Christ,* **separated** *to the gospel of God.*Rom.1:1

*We thought it good to show the **signs** and **wonders***

that the high God has wrought. How great are his signs! and how mighty are his wonders! Dan.4:2-3

*We speak that **we do know** and testify that we have* seen. [We trust that you will] *receive our witness.*Jn. 3:11

Revelation of Jesus

*God...which does great things and unsearchable; marvelous things without number,*Job 5:8-9 *has **fulfilled his word** that he has commanded,*Lam.2:17 *and has in these last days spoken* Heb.1:2 afresh to *great multitudes of people which followed him* Mat.4:25 from many parts of the countries where we have proclaimed the Good News.

*It pleased God, who separated me from my mothers' womb, and called me by His grace, to reveal his Son in me, that I might **preach Him among the** **non-Christians of every nation.***Gal.1:15-16

*For Christ sent us to **preach the gospel:** not with wisdom of words, lest the cross of Christ should be made of none effect. For the **preaching of the cross** is to them that perish foolishness; but to us which are saved it is the power of God.*1Cor.1:17-18

*We certify you, that **the gospel** which is preached by us is not after man. For we neither received it of man, neither were we taught it, but by the **revelation of Jesus Christ.*** Gal.1:11-12

And we believe that ***the gospel of Christ** is **the power of God** to salvation to everyone that believes.* Rom.1:16

By Word and Deed

We have not ventured to [include in this "gospel"] *anything but what Christ has done through us to bring the* [non-Christians to believe on Christ] *by* **word** *and* **deed**, *by the* **power of signs and wonders**, *by the* **power of the Holy Spirit.**Rom.15:18-19ML

We believe that *God, who at various times and in different ways spoke in time past to the fathers by the prophets, has in these last days* **spoken to us** *by his Son Jesus*Heb.1:1-2 *whom God anointed with the Holy Ghost and with power: who went about* **doing good**, *and* **healing all** *that were oppressed of the devil;*Ac.10:38 *and* **we are his witnesses.**Ac.5:32

This Jesus of Nazareth was a man **approved of God** *among people by* **miracles** *and* **wonders** *and* **signs** *which God did by him.*Ac.2:22

Crucified but Risen

But jealous religious opposers *reasoned in their hearts* [and said], *this man speaks blasphemies.*Mk.2:6-7 *And there was much murmuring among the people concerning him: some said, he deceives the people,*Jn.7:12 *and they took counsel together to put him to death.*Jn.11:53

They finally laid hold on Jesus and led him away to Caiaphas the high priest, where the scribes and the elders were assembled, and all the council sought false witnesses against him, to **put him to death.**Mat.26:57,59

*They cried out, saying, Crucify him, crucify him. He ought to die, **because he makes himself the Son of God.**[Jn.19:16] And they killed the Prince of life, whom **God raised** from the dead; whereof we are witnesses;[Ac.3:15] God made of that same Jesus, who was crucified, both Lord and Christ.[Ac.2:36]*

*He **died** for our sins according to the scriptures, and he was **buried**, and he **rose again** the third day according to the scriptures.[1Cor.15:3-4]*

In fact, *he **showed himself alive** after his passion by many **infallible proofs**, being seen of them forty days.*[Ac.1:3]

*He was seen of **Cephas**, then of **the twelve**: After that, he was seen of about **five hundred at once**; after that, he was seen of **James**; then of **all the apostles**. He was seen of **Paul also**.*[1Cor.15:5-8]

And **He was seen of me** when He appeared to me in my bedroom. In like manner **He was seen of Daisy** as He came to her and told her to preach the gospel. He was also seen by our daughter, LaDonna who appeared to her on the day that she accepted Him as her Savior.

Then as we have gone *to all the world to preach the gospel,*[Mk.16:15] Jesus has appeared to **one** or to **several people** in almost every crusade we have ever conducted. In Thailand, **over one hundred people** saw our Lord at one time, in the same meeting, and *the people with one accord gave heed to the things which we spoke and there was great joy in that city.*[Ac.8:6,8]

And best of all, Jesus promised, *Lo I am with YOU alway, even to the end of the world.*[Mat.28:20]

So we believe that this same Jesus is **with us** wherever we go, because after *he was parted from them, and carried up into heaven*[Lu.24:51] *they went forth, and preached every where, **the Lord working with them, confirming the word with signs following.***[Mk.16:20] We have literally experienced this in over a hundred nations. *He has said, I will never leave you, or forsake you.*[Heb.13:5]

He Chose Us

So we *have not chosen Christ, but **He has chosen us**, and **ordained us**, that we should go and bring forth fruit, and that our fruit shall remain: that whatever we ask of the Father in Christ's name, He may give it to us.*[Jn.15:16]

We believe that *if we abide in Christ, and if his words abide in us, we can ask what we will, and **it shall be done to us.***[Jn.15:7]

Christ has clearly said: *if we believe on him, the works that he does **we shall do also**...and whatever we shall ask in his name, he will do, that the Father may be glorified in the Son.*[Jn.14:12-13]

So, *this is the confidence that we have in him, that, if we ask **anything** according to God's will [or word of promise], he hears us: and if we know that he hears us, whatever we ask, we know that **we have** the petitions that we desire of him.*[1Jn.5:14-15]

We Are His Witnesses

We have gone to the world, during over six decades, *and preached **Christ** to them.*[Ac.8:5]

We believe *that this is a faithful saying and worthy of all acceptation, that **Christ came** to this world **to save sinners.**[1Tim.1:15]* So we tell the world that *God sent not his Son to the world to **condemn** the world; but that the world through him might be saved,*[Jn.3:17] because the great fact is that *the Son of Man is come to **seek** and to **save** that which was lost.*[Lu.19:10]

As we reach out to minister to these millions, we are always occupied *preaching the kingdom of God, and teaching those things which concern **the Lord Jesus Christ**, with all confidence:*[Ac.28:31] how *he was wounded for **our** transgressions, he was bruised for **our** iniquities: the chastisement of our peace was upon him: and with his stripes we are healed.*[Isa.53:5]

Great multitudes come together to hear, and to be healed by the Lord of their infirmities,[Lu.5:15] and we teach them how *Christ **healed all** that were sick: that it might be fulfilled which was spoken by Isaiah the prophet who said, himself took out infirmities, and bore **our** sicknesses.*[Mat.8:16-17]

*And believers are the more added to the Lord, **multitudes** both of men and women.*[Ac.5:14]

These *multitudes bring the sick to the streets* [or fields or race courses or stadiums or ball parks where we preach], *and lay them on beds and couches.*

Ac.5:15 We preach to them that *as many as receive Christ* receive power to become children of God,Jn.1:12-13 and that *as many as touch him* are made perfectly whole.Mk.6:56

There are also multitudes [who come from] *the cities round about to* [our crusades and miracle evangelism festivals], *bringing sick folks, and them which are vexed with unclean spirits: and they are healed,*Ac.5:16 as they come to understand that *God forgives **all** iniquities, and he heals all **diseases.***Psa.103:3

We are witnesses of these things; and so is also the Holy Ghost;Ac.5:32 God also **bearing US witness** both with **signs** and **wonders,** and **divers miracles.**Heb.2:4

*We walk by **faith,** and not by **sight,***2Cor.5:7 knowing well *that without faith, it is* **impossible** *to please God;*Heb.11:6 that *the just shall* **live by faith,**Rom.1:17 because *Christ is the end of the law for righteousness to* **everyone that believes.**Rom.10:4

Our Principle Message

Our number one message is: *God so loved the world that he gave his only begotten Son, that **whoever believes** in him shall **not perish,** but shall **have everlasting life.***Jn.3:16 We want everyone in each multitude to know that *Jesus is the* [only] **way,** *the* [only] **truth** *and the* [only] **life;** [that] *no one can come to God except through him;*Jn.14:6 that *he is able to* **save to the uttermost** *them that come to God by him, because he is alive and makes intercession for them.*Heb.7:25

343

As *great multitudes come together* **to hear**, *and* **to be healed** *by Christ of their infirmities,*^{Lu.5:15} we know that *faith* [can only] *come* [to them] *by hearing, and hearing by the **word of God.***^{Rom.10:17} So we constantly **teach** and **preach** *the gospel of the kingdom.*^{Mat.4:23}

Often, as we are teaching, *the power of the Lord is* **present to heal.** *The whole multitude seeks to touch Jesus: because virtue goes out of Him,* [through His Word], *and* **He heals them.**^{Lu.6:19}

They bring **sick** *folks taken with* **divers diseases** *and* **torments**, *and those* **possessed with devils**, *and those that are* **lunatic**, *and those with* **palsy**, *and Christ heals them.*^{Mat.4:24}

In Christ's name, we charge many *deaf and dumb spirits to* **come out** *and to enter no more into the people.* ^{Mk.9:25} Sometimes, *when the evening comes, they bring many that are possessed with devils; and we* **cast out the spirits of infirmity with his word**, *and Christ heals them.*^{Mat.8:16} Often it seems that *the whole city comes out to meet Jesus.*^{Mat.8:34}

Our message is: *For with God* **all things are possible.**^{Mk.10:27} *According to your faith, it* **will** *be done to you.*^{Mat.9:29} *If you can believe,* **all things are possible to anyone who believes.**^{Mk.9:23} **Whatever** *things you desire, when you pray,* **believe** *that you* **receive** *them and you shall have them.*^{Mk.11:24}

We believe Jesus Christ is our principle message because He said, *and I, if I be lifted up, will draw all people to me.*^{Jn.12:32} The apostle Paul said, *For other* *foundation can no one lay than that that is laid, which is **Jesus Christ.**1Cor.3:11* We concluded long ago: *God forbid that we should ever glory, save in the **cross of our Lord Jesus Christ** by whom the world is crucified to us, and us to the world.*Gal.6:14

Full of Faith and Power

We never fail to emphasize that *Jesus Christ is the same **yesterday** and **today** and **forever**,*Heb.13:8 and that this was the faith of those *who had spoken to us the word of God: and it was they whose faith we should follow, considering the end of their conversation.*Heb.13:7

Barnabas was an example to follow. When he preached, *much people was added to the Lord,*Ac.11:24 *for he was a good man and **full of the Holy Ghost and of faith.***Ac.11:24

Stephen was another example to emulate because *he was **full of faith and power**, and did great **wonders** and **miracles** among the people.*Ac.6:8

That is why we believe miracles should follow our ministry; they **attract** and **convince** *much people to be added to the Lord.*Ac.11:24

When we enter a city, we *speak **boldly** in the name of the Lord, who always gives testimony to the word of his grace, and He always grants **signs** and **wonders** to be done.*Ac.14:3

*The hand of the Lord is always with us: and great numbers believe, and **turn to the Lord.***Ac.11:21

As we preach Christ to them, the people with one accord give heed to the things which we speak, **hearing and seeing the miracles** *which are done, and there is always great joy in each city.*Ac.8:6-8

Confirming His Word

As we speak of the things we have seen and heard, Ac.4:20 *we perceive that many have faith to be healed* [and we command the lame:] **Stand up on your feet and walk.**Ac.14:9-10

Often they **immediately** *rise, take up their bed, and go their way to their house, as the multitude is amazed and glorifies God, saying, We never saw it on this fashion.*Mk.2:11-12 Sometimes those who are healed **leap up** *and* **stand** *and* **walk,** *and go to the churches* **walking** *and* **leaping** *and* **praising God,** *and the people see them walking and praising God.*Ac.3:8-9

Unbelievers are often heard to say: *What shall we do? For that indeed a* **notable miracle** *has been done is manifest to all that dwell in the city; and* **we cannot deny it.**Ac.4:1

It is always evident that *the Lord is working with us,* **confirming his word** *with signs following.*Mk.16:20 Almost always, *many of them that hear the word believe: and the number of them is usually* **thousands.**Ac.4:4 *Believers are the more added to the Lord,* **multitudes** *both of men and women,*Ac.5:14 *and all glorify God for what is done.*Ac.4:21

They See the Miracles

We implicitly obey the words of our Lord: *Go to all the world, and preach the gospel to every creature and these signs always **follow** them that believe. In his name we cast out devils. They* [the sick people present] *lay their hands* [on their own bodies where they are sick] *and they recover.*[Mk.16:15,17-18]

The Lord has *cured many of their infirmities and **plagues**, and of **evil spirits**; and to many that were **blind**, he gives sight.*[Lu.7:21] People are *loosed from their **infirmities** whom Satan has bound for many years.*[Lu.13:12,16]

Some are **immediately** *cured and they glorify God.*[Lu.13:13] Others **at the same hour begin to mend,**[Jn.4:52] and some, like the lepers, are healed **as they go.**[Lu.17:14]

The faith of thousands is always united with us as we pray for God to confirm His word *by stretching forth his hand to heal, by granting **signs and wonders** to be done in the name of his holy child Jesus.*[Ac.4:29-30]

All the people rejoice for all the glorious things that are done.[Lu.13:17] *And great multitudes follow him, because **they see the miracles** which he does on them which are diseased.*[Jn.6:2]

Those who are healed are told to *go home to their friends, and to tell them how great things **the Lord has done** for them, and has had compassion on them. And* *they always publish in the area how great things Jesus has done for them: and all the people marvel* ^{Mk.5:19-20} and are *amazed and they glorify God, saying, **we never saw it on this fashion.***^{Mk.2:12}

The Gods Are Come Down

There are always some, who when they see the miracles say, of a truth these people are gods; *the gods are come down to us in the likeness of people,* ^{Ac.14:11} *which when we hear of, we say,* We cannot heal! We are not gods! *We are only people of like passions with you, and we preach to you that you should **turn to the living God.***^{Ac.14:15} *And with these sayings, we can scarcely restrain the people from worshipping us.*^{Ac.14:18}

We always explain to them *that from* [America], *round about to* [Asia and in over 100 nations] *we have fully preached **the gospel of Christ,***^{Rom.15:19} *making the* [non-Christians] *obedient, by **word** and **deed**, through **mighty signs and wonders** by the **power of the spirit of God.***^{Rom.15:18-19}

The Gospel Is Power

Furthermore, we emphasize that we have *tried to preach **where Christ is not named** lest we build on another person's foundation.*^{Rom.15:20}

We *come not to the people with excellency of speech or of wisdom, and we determine not to know anything among them, **save Jesus Christ and him crucified.***

Our *speech and our preaching is not with enticing*

words of human wisdom, but in the **demonstration of the Spirit and of power.**

We teach *that one's faith should not stand in the wisdom of people but* **in the power of God.**[1Cor.2:1-5]

We *declare the gospel by which people are saved, how that Christ* **died** *for our sins according to the scriptures; and that he was* **buried**, *and that he* **rose again** *the third day.*[1Cor.15:1-4]

We believe this is vital to proclaim because *if Christ be not risen, then is* **our preaching vain**, *and* **your faith is vain**, *and we are* **false witnesses** *of Christ.*[1Cor.15:13-15]

Two Cardinal Facts

The death and resurrection of Christ sets Christianity apart from all religions so it is vital that people believe these two facts because salvation depends on them:

1) *If you shall confess with your mouth* **the Lord Jesus**, *and* 2) *believe in your heart that God has* **raised him from the dead**, [those are the conditions on which] **you will be saved**. *For* 1) *with the heart you believe* [in the righteousness of Christ] *and* 2) *with your mouth, you make confession to salvation.*[Rom.10:9-10]

Believing those two facts, **whoever** *shall call on the name of the Lord shall be saved.*[Rom.10:13]

But since *faith comes by hearing the word of God,* [Rom.10:17], *how shall people hear without a preacher?* [Rom.10:14] That is why *we are ready to preach the gospel,*

Rom.1:15 *we are **not ashamed** of the gospel,*Rom.1:16 *and we **declare** the gospel.*1Cor.15:1

We can say that *we have preached the gospel of God **freely**,*2Cor.11:7 because we will not ***pervert*** the gospel.Gal.1:7

Unsearchable Riches

Whenever *false brethren have tried to spy out our liberty in Christ Jesus so that they might bring us into bondage, we give no place or subjection, no, not even for an hour, that the **truth of the gospel** might continue.*Gal.2:4-5

We consistently teach and preach that *according to the **truth of the gospel**, [people] must believe in Jesus Christ, that they might be **justified by the faith of Christ** and not by their works.*Gal.2:14,16

We believe that *after people hear the **word of truth**, the **gospel of salvation**, [they are] **sealed** with the holy Spirit of promise,*Eph.1:13 *and that they become **heirs** of the same body, and **partakers** of the promise in Christ by the gospel, whereof we are made ministers, according to the gift of the grace of God given to us by the effectual working of his power. To us is this grace given, that we should preach among the [**non**-Christians] the unsearchable **riches of Christ**.*Eph.3:6-9

*Our gospel came not [nor do we proclaim it] in word only, but also in **power**, and in the **Holy Ghost**, and in **much assurance**.*1Th.1:5

Entrusted with the Gospel

We consider that *we have been allowed of God to be* **put in TRUST with the gospel**, *and so we speak it; not as pleasing people, but God.*[1Th.2:4]

Indeed *we labor night and day,* **preaching the gospel** *of God, holy and just and unblameably behaving ourselves, so that we always walk worthy of God, who has* **called us** *to his kingdom and glory.*[1Th.2:9-10,12]

We believe that *the word of the Lord* **endures forever.** *And this is the word by which the* **gospel** *is preached.*[1Pet.1:25]

We know that *if anyone is* **in Christ**, *he or she is a new creature: old things are passed away, behold all things are become new.*[2Cor.5:17]

We *declare before all the people*[Lu.8:47] that **in Christ alone** *is life;*[Jn.1:4] *that God has given to us eternal life, and that this life is* **in his Son.** *Whoever has the Son* **has life**; *and whoever has not the Son of God* **has not life.**[1Jn.5:11-12] *As many as* **receive Jesus Christ**, *to them he gives power to become the children of God.*[Jn.1:12]

We say: *These things have we spoken to you that you may* **know** *that you* **have** *eternal life, and that you may* **believe** *on the name of the Son of God,*[1Jn.5:11-13] because *there is* **no other name** *under heaven given among us, by which we may be* **saved.**[Ac.4:12] *And with many other words do we testify and exhort, saying,*[Ac.2:40] **whoever** *shall call on the name of the Lord shall be* **saved.**[Rom.10:13]

We constantly recount the miracles wrought by Christ on earth, as examples for **anyone today**, and we tell them that *these miracles are written that the people may believe that Jesus is the Christ, the Son of God, and that believing, they may have LIFE through his name.*[Jn.20:31]

Winning with Christ

The reactions to our ministry are always varied. Some of the *priests of the temples*, [and even some of the Christian religious leaders] *are grieved that we teach the people, and preach through Jesus the resurrection* [Ac.4:1-2] from a dead life of sin to a **new life in Christ.**

In fact, in one of our crusades abroad, the magistrate closed the meeting in order to appease a group *which believed not. They were moved with envy and took certain lewd fellows of the baser sort, and gathered a company, and tried to set all the city in an uproar.* [Ac.17:5]

*However **many** of them which heard the word in that city **believed**,*[Ac.4:4] *and of the devout* [Hindus, Muslims and people of many religions] *a great multitude, and of the women not a few.* [Ac.17:4]

In most of our crusades abroad, *many of them which hear the word believe,*[Ac.4:4] while *others are filled with indignation,*[Ac.5:17] and *doubt* [about the extent to which] *this will grow.*[Ac.5:24] But we always take the position that *we ought to obey **God** rather than people.* [Ac.5:29]

So we continually *sound out the word of the Lord,* ^1Th.1:8 preaching that *in the name of Jesus Christ of Nazareth* [people can] *rise up and walk;* ^Ac.3:6 that *his name through faith in his name* ^Ac.3:16 can make people strong.

Of course, *the multitude of those who believe are of one heart and of one soul,* ^Ac.4:32 *and the hand of the Lord is **always** with us.* ^Ac.11:21

We believe *the Holy Ghost has fallen on us **the same** as it fell* [on those] *at the beginning* [in Jerusalem], ^Ac.11:15 and we are thankful that *great grace is upon us.* ^Ac.4:33

Let God Be True

But people sometimes *stagger at the promises of God through **unbelief.*** ^Rom.4:20

Some seem to have fear and unbelief, and *think that it is a thing **incredible** that God should* [perform miracles in this age]. ^Ac.26:8

Some think that mass evangelism was alright in the book of Acts, but that it is not God's program for this day. There are people who even believe that miracles were only for the Apostles. Of course through their unbelief no *mighty works* are done among them, ^Mk.6:5 and the Lord, no doubt, *marvels because of their **unbelief.*** ^Mk.6:6

We feel, however, that *even if some do not believe, their unbelief should not make the faith of God without effect.* [We feel that we should] *let **God be true**, but every person a liar.* ^Rom.3:3-4

In spite of these reactions here and there, *we continue to this day, witnessing both to small and great, saying none other things than those which the prophets said should come: That Christ should **suffer** and that he should rise from the dead and should **show light** to the* Ac.26:22-23 non-Christians.

We proclaim that Jesus Christ *himself took **our** infirmities, and bore **our** sicknesses,* Mat.8:17 and that *with his stripes **we** are healed* Isa.53:5; and that He, *himself bore **our** sins in his own body on the cross so that we, being dead to sins, should **live to righteousness**.* 1Pet. 2:24

In non-Christian nations, we have even faced leaders who consider our ministry *a sect that is spoken against.* Ac.28:22

But wherever people **accept the gospel**, they *fear, lest a promise being left, any of them should seem to come short of it.* Heb.4:1 They rejoice that *the gospel is preached to them* [but they regret that] *the word preached does not profit* [those who believe not], *not being **mixed with faith** in them that heard it.* Heb.4:2

Notable Miracles

So as it was in the days of the Bible, we observe that it is the same in our day: Some would not believe, but those who ***believe**, see the glory of God,* Jn.11:40 and we continue to *heal the sick, to cleanse the lepers, to raise the dead and to cast out devils* Mat.10:8 wherever we announce the gospel, since Jesus commanded it and has given us *power over all the power of the enemy.*[Lu.10:19; Mk.3:14-15]

The healing ministry of Christ is of great importance because miracles cause *the people to **run together**, greatly wondering.*[Ac.3:11] Miracles cause the people to ***give heed*** *to the things that we teach.*[Ac.8:6]

Notable miracles [are done which are] *manifest to all them that are in* [the cities wherever we go], *and no one can deny them.*[Ac.4:16]

As great miracles take place, *many see them, and* ***turn to the Lord.***[Ac.9:35] *And as* [these things become] *known throughout the area, many **believe** in the Lord.*[Ac.9:42]

When those healed testify, *others also, which have diseases come, and are healed.*[Ac.28:9]

Only seldom do we encounter those who are *filled with envy and speak against these things.*[Ac.13:45] Most people *are **glad**, and **glorify** the word of the Lord.*[Ac.13:48]

Tens of thousands *are **amazed** and **glorify** God, saying: We never saw it on this fashion.*[Mk.2:12]

It is wonderful when *great multitudes come, having with them those who are lame, blind, maimed, and many others, and cast them down at Jesus' feet; **and He heals them:** Insomuch that the multitudes wonder, when they see the dumb to speak, the maimed to be whole, the lame to walk, and the blind to see: and they glorify the God of Israel.*[Mk.15:30-31]

Thank God, *believers are the more* **added to the Lord**, *multitudes both of men and women.*Ac.5:13

The word of God **increases**; *and the number of the disciples* **multiply** *in each area greatly; and a* **great company** *of* [those of non-Christian religions] *are obedient to the faith,*Ac.6:7 *so mightily* **grows** *the word of God and* **prevails.**Ac.19:20 Also *the name of the Lord Jesus is* **magnified.**Ac.19:17

If God Said It, He Will Do It

These things *now have* **WE seen** *with our eyes,*Zech. 9:8 as we constantly teach that *there has not failed* **one word** *of all God's good promise which He has promised.*1Kg.8:56

We emphasize that *God is not a man, that he should lie; neither the Son of man, that he should* **repent**: *If he has said it,* **he will do it**. *If he has spoken,* **he will make it good,**Num.23:19 because He has said, *I am the Lord: I will speak, and the word that I shall speak* **shall come to pass**; *I will say the word, and* **will perform it.**Eze. 12:25 He says, *the word which I have spoken* **shall be done.**Eze.12:28

We constantly teach the multitudes in our meetings the faithfulness of God to fulfill His word. *The Lord will do the thing that he has promised.*Isa.38:7 He says, *Yes, I have spoken it, and* **I will also bring it to pass**; *I have purposed it, and* **I will also do it.**Isa.46:11 We love to assure the people that *heaven and earth shall pass away, but Christ's words* **shall not** *pass away.*Mat.24:35

Receive Our Witness

To teach and convince these masses about Jesus Christ, God always keeps us *full of faith and **power**, [then He can do] *great **wonders** and **miracles** among the people.*^{Ac.6:8}

We report what **we** have seen Jesus do, like John's disciples reported what they had seen Him do: *The **blind** receive their sight, and the **lame** walk, the **lepers** are cleansed, and the **deaf** hear, the **dead** are raised up, and the **poor** have the gospel preached to them.*^{Mat.11:5}

Truly, the vital message of our Lord is, *The time is fulfilled, and the kingdom of God is at hand: repent and **believe the gospel**,*^{Mk.1:15} *because if the mighty works which were done in your days had been done in many previous generations, they would have repented long ago.*^{Mat.11:21}

Now Is the Time

We urge you to **believe** *on the Lord Jesus Christ* [right now] *and you shall be **saved**, and your house.*^{Ac.16:31}

Since **now** *is the accepted time, and now is the day of salvation,*^{2Cor.6:2} you can *repent and be converted, that your sins may be blotted out* ^{Ac.3:19} by **looking to Jesus** *the author and finisher of your faith* ^{Heb.12:2} who *has redeemed **you** to God,*^{Rev.5:9} *because he loved **you** and washed **you** from **your** sins in his own blood* ^{Rev.1:5} *of the new testament, which is shed for many for the **remission of sins**.*^{Mat.26:28}

It is wonderful to know that after *Christ died for the ungodly,*[Rom.5:6] *God, having raised up his Son,* **sent him to bless you**, *in turning you away from your iniquities.*[Ac.3:26]

God commends his love toward you, in that, while you were still a sinner, **Christ died for you.** *Now being justified by his blood,* **you will be saved** *from all wrath.*[Rom.5:8-9]

So reckon yourself **dead indeed to sin**, *but* **alive to God** *through Jesus Christ your Lord, for the wages of sin is* **death**; *but the gift of God is* **eternal life** *through Jesus Christ our Lord.*[Rom.6:11,23]

You *are in Christ Jesus, who of God is made* **to you** *wisdom, and righteousness, and sanctification, and redemption.*[1Cor.1:30]

The life of Jesus is also made manifest in **your mortal flesh,** [2Cor.4:10] *because* **your body** *is the temple of the Holy Ghost* [1Cor.6:19] *and you are a member of Christ's* **body**, *of his* **flesh**, *and of his* **bones.**[Eph.5:30]

His Desire for You

His desire is not only to **forgive all of** **your** *iniquities,* [but also to] *heal all of* **your** *diseases* [Psa.103:3] *because, himself took* **your** *infirmities and bore* **your** *sicknesses* [Mat.8:17] *the same as he bore* **your** *sins in his own body on the cross.*[1Pet.2:24]

Since Christ bore **your** sins, **you** can have *remission of sins* [Mat.26:28] NOW. Since He bore your sicknesses, *by his stripes* **you** *are healed* [1Pet.2:24] NOW.